The 1908 Olympics

Keith Baker

SPORTS
BOOKS

Published by SportsBooks Ltd

Copyright: Keith Baker ©
February 2008

SportsBooks Limited
PO Box 422
Cheltenham
GL50 2YN
United Kingdom
Tel: 01242 256755
Fax: 01242 254694
e-mail   randall@sportsbooks.ltd.uk
Website   www.sportsbooks.ltd.uk

Cover designed by Alan Hunns

Photographs in plate section from PA Photos

A CIP catalogue record for this book is available from the British Library.

ISBN 9781899807 61 1
Printed by Creative Print and Design, Wales

This book is dedicated to those who made the 1908 Olympic Games possible and to those who took part in them.

Contents

	Acknowledgements	ix
	Introduction	1
1	London prepares for the Games	9
2	The Games Begin	22
3	Trouble Ahead	31
4	Trouble Afoot	36
5	The Loneliness of a 400 metres runner	41
6	Marathon Drama	51
7	2,000 men – 36 women	62
8	America fumes, Britain blusters	72
9	The Olympians	82
10	Man of Affairs and Lover of Games	85
11	Soldier Athlete	95
12	The Bohola Boy	101
13	The Man who upset the King	110
14	Dorando and Johnny	115
15	Everything a Runner should be	127
16	From "dirty water" to Olympic gold	137
17	Skating Pioneer	143
18	From Sydney to Hollywood	148
19	The best and worst of Games	158
	Statistics	167
	Annotated Bibliography	175
	About the author	179

ACKNOWLEDGEMENTS

O ne hundred years ago, with barely two years' notice, London staged the Games that were to revitalise the Olympics of the modern era. The spectacle they provided, and their dramatic events, continue to attract the interest and imagination not only of sports scholars and writers, but of ordinary sports fans throughout the world. In writing this book I have been greatly helped by the large amount of published material contributed over the years by innumerable writers, statisticians, newspaper reporters and others on the Olympic movement and on the London Games of 1908 in particular. I owe a general debt of gratitude to them all, but especially to Theodore Cook's meticulous Official Report, and to Bill Mallon's and Ian Buchanan's masterly publication on the events of the 1908 Games, both of which have proved invaluable sources of reference.

I have been fortunate enough to live relatively near to the excellent British Library at Boston Spa and I am deeply grateful to the library staff there for their professionalism and friendliness with which they traced and provided material for me on countless occasions. Similarly, my thanks are due to staff at the Public Libraries in the cities of Sheffield and Oldham, to those at the Colindale Newspaper

Library, and to the staff of the British Olympic Association. Without the help of all the above, this book would never have come to fruition. If in using any of the material provided any copyright has been infringed, the lapse has been wholly unintentional.

As regards individuals, I am particularly indebted to Rob Evans, Richard Ashdown, Deidre MacDonagh, David Price, Bernard Edge and Michael Stewart for their encouragement, support and advice, and for the personal information they provided for me on some of the heroes of the 1908 Games. Most of all, I owe more than can be ever repaid to my wife, Sarah, for her invaluable comments on the manuscript in draft and to her love and encouragement throughout the project.

INTRODUCTION

The Olympic Games have been rightly described as the "Mount Everest of Sport." No other sporting event has more prestige or is given more publicity. Every four years young men and women representing virtually all the nations of the world come together to compete against one another in a great variety of sports.

The growth of the Games has been phenomenal. In 1896, when the first of the "modern" Olympics was held in Athens, there were only three hundred athletes from eleven countries. When the Olympics returned to Athens in 2004, some eleven thousand athletes competed from more than two hundred countries. Despite the cost of the Games, their commercialisation and razzmatazz, and the controversies that seem inevitably to surround them, the Olympics mean something special to people and are extraordinarily popular.

The lofty ideals, such as the promotion of "harmony and goodwill" and "universal peace", with which the modern Olympics were launched more than one hundred years ago, may now have little resonance. But millions of people are drawn to the Games as a singularly human institution, a great and sometimes beautiful spectacle, where emotions run high and heroic deeds are played out before them.

The 1908 Olympics

The ancient Olympic Games are regarded as starting at Olympia, Greece in 776 BC and were discontinued in AD 393 by the Roman Emperor Theodosius the Great when he outlawed all Greece's religious landmarks and its pagan ceremonies. Towards the end of the nineteenth century, it was mainly through the vision, enthusiasm and efforts of a Frenchman named Baron de Coubertin that the Olympic movement was resurrected. He was able to promote enough interest in the idea for the first Olympiad of the modern era to be held in Athens in 1896. Before the Olympics came to London in 1908, three more Games were held, in Paris in 1900, St Louis in 1904, and the so-called "intercalated" or interim Games of Athens in 1906.

The opening ceremony of the 1896 Athens Games on Easter Sunday drew huge crowds. The Games could hardly be considered an international event since two-thirds of the competitors were Greek, together with a mere twenty-one Germans, nineteen Frenchman, fourteen Americans and eight Britons, together with a smattering of other nationalities.

The Greek spectators, hungry for success, grew more angry and frustrated as one event after another was won by the Americans. It was a Greek shepherd called Spyridon Loues who came to their rescue when he won the marathon. A devout man, he was said to have spent most of the previous evening in prayer and had fasted the entire day before the race.

The popular response to Loues' victory, and the national celebrations which followed, were so great that they created just the momentum needed for the Olympic experiment to feel confident enough to move on to its next selected venue – Paris.

Unfortunately, the Paris Games of 1900 were not a success. They took place over a period of two months, and since they were arranged as a peripheral part of a World Fair, they were hardly noticed by visitors. Athletes from twenty countries competed, but most of the competitors were said to have treated the Games as a huge joke. Competitions were held in dismal facilities and were poorly organised.

The track and field events were held in the Bois de Boulogne. Races took place on the grass because the French did not want to disfigure the grass with a cinder track. The discus and javelin throws got caught in the trees which the French refused to cut down. The swimmers and divers were compelled to compete in the polluted waters of the Seine. Swimming the river downstream, the Australian swimmer, Frederick Lane, was swept along so fast by the current that he smashed the official 200 metres record by thirteen seconds!

The 1904 Games held in St Louis, USA, were equally disappointing, and generally regarded as the worst in the history of the Olympic movement. They have been described as being "bathed in nationalism, ethnocentrism, controversy, confusion, and bad taste". (Findling & Pelle – *Historical*

Dictionary of the Modern Olympic Movement). Faced with a transatlantic voyage and a 1,000 mile train ride, most Europeans decided not to attend what some suspected to be a wilderness settlement menaced by Indians. British journalists covering the event claimed later that their most abiding memory was that "the sole fare on the menu was buffalo meat"(Guttman – *The Olympics*).

Only nine nations were represented and the Games turned out to be little more than a United States sports fixture. Americans won twenty-two out of the twenty-three track and field events. Once more, it was the marathon that provided the real excitement. The American athlete Fred Lorz thrilled the home crowd by finishing well ahead of anyone else in the race but the euphoria soon evaporated when he was disqualified for travelling part of the way on a truck.

After the disappointments of Paris and St Louis, the whole Olympic movement might well have ground to a halt. However, a group of Greek sports supporters, remembering the relative success of the 1896 Games, decided to mount another bid. They set about persuading the International Olympic Committee (IOC§) to agree to Greece holding in Athens what became known as the Intercalated (Interim) Olympic Games of 1906. In fact these Games were something of a sop to the Greeks who were bitter about the refusal of the IOC to accept their proposal to make Greece the permanent home of the Olympic Games. De Coubertin, who effectively dominated the committee, remained insistent that the chance to hold the Games should be shared among the large capitals of the world.

Although the 1906 Games, therefore, have never been recognised officially as "Olympic" Games, they were the first truly international event held under IOC auspices. They were much better organised than the two previous Olympiads. Twenty nations sent nearly nine hundred athletes to Athens. Competition was keen and public support good. Despite shortcomings, such as a lack of competition rules and accusations of partiality among the judges, the 1906 Games were considered a success. They had the effect of rekindling public and national interest in the Olympic concept.

The IOC agreed with Baron de Coubertin that it would be very appropriate for the fourth Olympiad of 1908 to be celebrated in Rome – the Eternal City. Italy eagerly welcomed the opportunity to demonstrate its credentials as a truly major European power and accepted the invitation. Unfortunately, in 1906 Mount Vesuvius erupted, and such was the damage and devastation caused, that the Italians asked to be relieved of the responsibility of staging the Games for financial reasons. Great Britain was the only country that seemed to have the wherewithal to rescue the 1908 Games at such desperately short notice, and the IOC turned to it for help. In November 1906 a letter was sent to the IOC stating that Britain was prepared to take over the Games.

The British responded to the enormous challenge of staging the 1908 Olympics with widely-praised drive and efficiency. With barely two years' notice and with limited resources, the organisers managed to stage the best-organised Games and the largest and most representative gathering of athletes ever before seen. However, there were also eruptions in London of a very different kind than those that had affected Rome.

They were scarred by a bitter round of disputes based mainly on an intense rivalry between the British and Americans – the so-called Battle of Shepherd's Bush. Consequently the London Games have gone down as one of the most controversial and dramatic in Olympic history.

This book has two main objectives. First, to describe the achievements of the London Games and its excitement and drama. It sets out to capture the major controversies that occurred, the reasons for them and their repercussions. It is not therefore a book of reference, a complete history of the entire 1908 Games, or of all its relevant statistical information.

The second objective relates to the people who in one way or another took part in the London Games. All Olympics have their heroes and owe much to many people. But the 1908 Games were particularly rich with the number of remarkable people whose sporting lives and achievements were truly memorable. Several will make a brief appearance on the pages of this book as events unfold. But there are some who stand out as deserving more attention.

Included therefore in this book is a series of personal portraits of some of those people – nine men and one woman – whose lives were touched deeply by the London Games, and who were never quite the same again. They came from widely different backgrounds, cultures, countries and sports. All were heroes in their own way, although not all Olympic champions. The Games launched a few of them into unprecedented fame and fortune as sporting superstars. For others, life thereafter was an anticlimax as they sunk into obscurity, and for some life came to be cruelly cut short.

Chapter 1

London prepares for the Games

*"The curtain descended on the Tiber's stage
and rose soon after on that of the Thames."
– Baron de Coubertin*

The Challenge

Once Italy had announced it was no longer able to stage the 1908 Games, Baron Pierre de Coubertin realised that the task of organising them with less than two years to go would be an extremely arduous one, and well beyond the scope of most countries. But he was determined that they should go ahead and in desperation he turned to Great Britain for help. Britain, after all, was regarded across the world as the motherland of sport, and had established a reputation for organising large-scale sporting events such as the Amateur Athletic Association (AAA) Championships, Wimbledon and the Henley Regatta.

He was fortunate that his eminent and influential British friend, Lord Desborough, shared his sporting enthusiasm and thought the idea an exciting one and just possible. In the event,

Desborough's organising ability, and his drive and determination, proved very influential in ensuring that all the preparatory work for the Games was completed on time.

A British Olympic Association was already in existence and Desborough, very ably assisted by its secretary, the Rev RS de Courcy Laffan, used this body as the basis for the organisation of the London Games. Its role and authority were quickly strengthened by turning it into the British Olympic Council (BOC). The Council proved to be remarkably effective and met virtually every fortnight over a period of two years.

The preparatory work was massive. Desborough and Laffan recognised that the planning for a programme consisting of more than one hundred events in twenty different forms of sport had to be meticulous.

The chaos of the earlier Games was still fresh in the memory. As well as no running track in Paris in 1900 there had been more competitors than spectators and the French and Americans spent the time arguing with one another.

The St Louis Games of 1904 had been even more of a disaster. Britain and France did not send one competitor and each day of competition was marred by fresh protest and counter protest. The BOC were determined that the London Games should set new standards of organisation and performance.

It was decided from the outset that all the preparatory tasks would be finished on time only by devolving most of the detailed work to each of the different British athletic and sporting associations representing the particular sport concerned. The membership of the BOC therefore was enlarged by including a representative of each sport participating in the Games. The associations immediately set about the daunting task of codifying the Olympic rules for all the competitions. Each sport required separate books of rules to be drawn up and agreed by more than twenty different nations. Once agreed, the rules were then translated into French and German and circulated to all the competing countries.

The stadium

The first and most important decision of the council was just where in London the main part of the Games should be held. There were several possible sites but the council had no money to invest in them. It was not able to turn to the Government for support for it was an accepted doctrine of the time that such projects should be carried out by private enterprise.

However, the council was extremely fortunate to find that an important Franco-British Exhibition was also to be held in 1908 and that work had already started on a massive one hundred and forty-acre site in Shepherd's Bush in west London. The brilliant white buildings making up the exhibition were being laid out in a cross pattern and soon attracted the name of the "White City".

When the organisers of the exhibition proposed that the Games should be held alongside the exhibition as had happened earlier at the Paris and St Louis Games, the council jumped at the offer. In fact, the terms proposed were remarkably attractive. The exhibition agreed to build the entire stadium at its own expense of "not less than £40,000", complete with all the facilities required. Moreover, it was agreed that the Council could also receive one quarter of the gross receipts of the Games.

Lord and Lady Desborough laid the first foundation stone for the White City Stadium on August 2nd 1907 and it was completed in the astonishing time of less than one year by a large labour force which worked by day and night. It made a most impressive sight. Built of five thousand tons of steel, it was the largest stadium constructed anywhere in the world and capable of holding one hundred and fifty thousand people, seventy thousand of whom could be seated.

The cinder running track, reckoned to be the finest in the world, measured three laps to the mile and contained no awkward corners. Outside it was a banked concrete cycle track. At one side of the stadium there was a swimming tank one hundred metres in length and with a maximum depth of fourteen feet for the high diving competition. Inside the running track there was a central arena for the field events, the association football, rugby football, hockey and lacrosse matches, and an area where the gymnastics and archery competitions could be held. Underneath the spectator terraces there were fourteen large dressing rooms for three thousand competitors, together with facilities for the police and ambulance services. No allowance was made for the serving of alcohol but there were five "temperance restaurants". It was reported that the stadium cost about £85,000 to build, although some sources suggest the actual cost was closer to £200,000.

By May 1908 the stadium was ready for competition. On May 14th, the Prince and Princess of Wales formally opened both the Franco-British Exhibition and the adjoining stadium which they dedicated to the cause of international sport. It was hardly a propitious start since on the day the stadium was declared open the rain fell continuously.

Although the Olympic organisers had undoubtedly secured a great stadium, they were still faced with raising the substantial sum of money needed to run the Games, plus all the hospitality expenses involved in an international event. In all, seven official banquets were organised in London by the BOC, attended by three thousand five hundred people.

Since there were no funds forthcoming from the government, the organisers were faced with a big financial problem. With just two weeks to go before the start of the Games, they were still short of £10,000. In desperation, Lord Desborough turned to the press baron, Lord Northcliffe, for help. Although Northcliffe personally was "not keen" on the Olympics, he reluctantly agreed to use his popular newspaper – the *Daily Mail* – to launch a final appeal to the public for support. In blatantly patriotic terms, the newspaper urged that, "Let the thousands who go to football matches in the winter; the thousands who watch cricket in the summer; the millions eager about all the games and exercises which all the year round form their greatest recreation – let them come forward now and contribute, in however small a measure, to the Ideal which England represents."

The response exceeded all expectations. Contributions simply poured in from all parts of Britain and overseas and from the rich and the poor. In just over a week over £12,000 had been subscribed, and the newspaper had to request its readers not to send any more money. The largest single individual contribution of £1,500 came from the famous strongman and bodybuilder of the time, Eugen Sandow. Out of the total sum for expenses of around £15,000, just over £5,300 was spent eventually on entertainment and hospitality. In the final outcome, the British Olympic Association finished with a remarkable profit of more than £6,000 on the Games.

The public attendance at the stadium during the first week was low, partly because the July weather was particularly wet and windy. But the Games had not been publicised well enough, and the entrance charges were initially set too high. On some days the attendance fell as low as ten thousand. Lord Desborough lamented, "Do they realise what they are missing? The greatest and most wonderful athletic meeting in the history of the world is in progress" (*The Sporting Life*). When at the beginning of the second week the entrance charges were reduced by half, and word got round about the events taking place, attendance improved markedly. By the time the marathon was run towards the end of the Games, the attendance in the stadium had risen to nearer ninety thousand.

The Programme

The programme for the Games had been approved by the International Olympic Committee (IOC) meeting at The Hague in the spring of 1907. As regards the sports to be included, it drew largely on the previous Games held in Paris, St Louis and Athens. They had laid down the basic principle that no competition should be approved which was not practised by several different nations. This meant that some of the sports initially proposed by the British such as cricket, baseball and pelota, were rejected.

Oddly, however, motorboat racing was included and seven boats raced for the three gold medals. In all, there were twenty-one different sports on the programme, far larger than had ever been included before. The 1908 Games were also the first time that events were spread around the country, so yachting, for example, was held at Ryde in the Isle of Wight, and the rowing at Henley. In total, some eight hundred officials were required to control the various events. Even then there were mutterings that the Games had become too big and should be shortened on future occasions.

The London Games took a significant step forward to increasing the participation of women. Women took part in the lawn tennis, which was reinstated at the Games having been dropped after 1900, and they also competed for the first time in the figure skating, which was introduced into the programme for the first time as a legitimate competitive event. A separate Winter Olympics was not held until Chamonix in 1924. Another addition, and one with considerable importance for the future, was the inclusion of a demonstration event for women gymnasts. All this was not entirely to the Baron de Coubertin's liking since he viewed the Olympics as essentially a sports festival for men and he would have preferred women to remain as admiring spectators.

In fact the 1908 Games were spread out over some six months to coincide with the Franco-British Exhibition held alongside the White City stadium. The Games were divided essentially into four phases. The first part of the so-called "Summer" Games began in late April and included activities such as golf, tennis and polo, then came the White City stadium events, primarily the track and field and swimming competitions. The rowing and yachting events, held at venues outside the stadium, followed and then came the so-called "Winter Games" including skating, association football, rugby and hockey.

Events at the stadium were on every weekday morning and afternoon until Saturday July 25th, when in the afternoon there was to be a "solemn presentation" of the prizes and commemorative medals. As a mark of goodwill, the British organisers adopted the metric measurement for the events, with the exception of the marathon.

The programme had been arranged so that the athletic races of 1500 metres and upwards, apart from the relays and marathon, would take place in the first week together with the cycling and gymnastics and some of the swimming events. All of the short distance races, the jumping and the remainder of the swimming were scheduled for the second week. With the permission of King Edward VII, the marathon was arranged to start from the private grounds of Windsor Castle on the afternoon of July 24th.

Rules and Regulations

The fair judging of all the various competitions had already emerged as a serious problem in earlier Games as there was no international agreement in place acceptable to all nations. Thus disputes over how juries should be drawn up, and charges of bias and incompetence, were legion. The IOC took what turned out to be an ill-fated decision when rather than appointing juries composed of different nationalities, they left the whole of the arrangements for judging the Games totally in the hands of the British governing association for each sport.

Such, it was confidently claimed, was the respect the world had for "the English love of fair play" (Official Report). De Coubertin himself supported the idea but it was one that he was to come to rue. Unfortunately, subsequent events showed that the famed British impartiality did not necessarily extend to the world of sport.

Another difficult problem facing the BOC was the definition of amateur status. At that time the Games were officially regarded as reserved strictly for the amateur competitor, the underlying principle being that an athlete loses his amateur status if he makes money out of the sport.

Unfortunately, getting a universal agreement on how the principle should be applied proved impractical, so each sport had to have a definition of its own. In practice the concept of the amateur was already proving something of a farce, not least when the French cycling team turned up in London with free cycles, free facilities and training expenses provided by British cycle firms seeking publicity! (Dobbs – *Edwardians at Play*)

The definition of the word "country" also taxed the Council. For the first time strict regulations were laid down regarding the nationality of the competitors. At previous Olympiads, members of any amateur athletic club in a country could represent that country irrespective of their nationality. Under the new regulations which the BOC drew up, only national-born or fully naturalised subjects of a country or of a sovereign state of which a country forms part were eligible to represent that "country." This definition adopted was to some extent forced upon the Council by what had been agreed in earlier Games, and became unfortunately another cause of contention among the competing nations.

It was agreed all contestants had to be certified by their national Olympic Committees. Restrictions on the number of competitors who could be entered were agreed and entry deadlines were established. It was no longer possible for anyone to simply turn up on the day and decide to compete. At the 1896 Games in Athens a British tourist, IP Boland had entered the tennis tournament on a whim and had won. And at St Louis in 1904, a Cuban postman hitch-hiked his way to the Games to compete in the marathon in what was reported to be his night shirt!

High Hopes

As the date of the Opening Ceremony grew nearer, the level of optimism rose. The organisers and other authorities predicted that the Games as a whole were going to be a resounding success and would set the standard as to how they should be organised in the future. The magazine, *The County*

Gentleman, predicted that "There is not the slightest doubt that it will be a series of gatherings the like of which the world has never seen." *The Times* declared its confidence that whoever won or lost would go away "satisfied and feeling that every opportunity has been given and every courtesy shown to him." Echoing those sentiments, the *Manchester Guardian* said that "England would suffer lasting disgrace if the Games of 1908 are not only equal in extent and interest to those which have preceded them, but so far superior as to develop a vast increase of zeal for these international gatherings".

Governments too had come to realise that the Games were now a major international event with the potential for much political impact. In 1908 political tensions across much of Europe were running particularly high. *The Times* announced that the Games "cannot but make for the prospects of world peace that ten of the world's civilised states should meet in friendly rivalry of the simplest and cleanest form of sport." The greatest modern gathering of athletes would, it was predicted, "be conducted from beginning to end in a spirit of perfect harmony," and people would be able to look back on the Games as having a "powerful impetus on the brotherhood of the world." And who, therefore, in British eyes was more fitted to open the fourth Olympiad than King Edward the Peacemaker?

Sadly, some of this idealism was painfully misplaced. The Games from day one fell far short of "perfect harmony." Even the Gods showed no favours, for the weather virtually throughout the Games was cold and wet. Only the day of the ill-fated Marathon was free from persistent rain, and then the weather was so hot and humid as to make long distance running highly uncomfortable. And as for the brotherhood of man, only six years later a World War broke out which took the lives of more than eight million young men.

Chapter 2

The Games Begin

"This was the most important international contest in the history of track and field events, for here were gathered the cream of the world's athletes; the champions of champions." – Caspar Witney, American sports writer.

Competition among nations

The preparations were complete and the athletes had assembled. Compared with the earlier Games, the number of foreign competitors taking part was "astoundingly large" (*The Times*, July 11th). There were around three thousand entries (although only just over two thousand actually competed), making the event much the greatest athletic gathering on record.

Great Britain had by far the largest number of competitors with seven hundred and thirty-six, made up of six hundred and ninety-seven men and thirty-nine women. The next largest were France with two hundred and eight, Sweden with one hundred and sixty-eight and the United States with one hundred and twenty-two.

The London Games marked a significant change from the earlier Olympiads in that for the first time there was not only to be competition among athletes but competition among nations. The outcome was predictable. National pride and prestige were at stake. For better or worse, from 1908 onwards nationalistic rivalry became an established feature of the Olympics.

Some countries made their intentions clear before they left for London. The United States team, selected after intensive national trials, was its strongest and largest yet. Its athletes made no secret that they were there to win most of the medals; their team captain, Martin Sheridan, boasted that "We will knock spots off the British".

The French Minister of War sent French athletes off to London with the reminder that their efforts "would be in vain were not the eyes of those young men always fixed on the flag which was the symbol of the Fatherland – and all the sacrifices France had the right to demand of her children" (*The Times* June 10th 1908).

Several countries had also appreciated the fact that sporting success demanded that their athletes should be carefully selected and prepared for the Games. In contrast to the British position, the French, German and Canadian governments all decided to fund their teams.

The large numbers of countries taking part made predictions of success very difficult, but as the Games grew closer there was inevitably much speculation in the press and elsewhere about who would be the winners and losers. Virtually all countries had one or two excellent athletes. A strong challenge was expected from Canada. Most observers agreed that the well-prepared Americans looked very powerful and would dominate the sprints, and the field events such as the discus, weight putting and javelin. It should be, predicted *The Sporting Life*, "a keen and mighty struggle between the United States and Great Britain."

Generally the selection of the British competitors had been received enthusiastically and there was "not the slightest doubt" that they would "pull off many of the prizes" (*The County Gentleman*). High hopes in particular were held for British chances in the 400 metres and the longer races, including the marathon, and in the relays and walking races.

The Opening Ceremony

On the afternoon of Monday July 13th 1908, the Games were officially declared open by King Edward VII, the patron of the Olympic Games, and himself an enthusiastic sportsman in his younger days. The day had dawned cloudy and wet and by mid morning the roadway to the Exhibition grounds had turned into a sea of liquid mud.

But this did not stop some forty thousand spectators making their way to the stadium. Only shortly before 3pm, when the King and his party left Buckingham Palace, did the rain relent.

On entering the stadium the King and Queen Alexandra drove to the royal box where the band, drums and pipes of the Scots Guards and soldiers from the Grenadier Guards were drawn up (*The Times* July 14th). They were received by Lord Desborough, Baron de Coubertin and members of the International and British Olympic Committees. Also present in the box were the Crown Prince and Princess of Greece, the Crown Prince and Princess of Sweden, King Haakon of Norway, and other distinguished representatives from Britain and overseas.

The box itself was situated in the centre of the west side of the stadium, directly opposite the stand displaying the flags of the competing nations and topped by a crown bearing the inscription, "Edward VII, Rex and Imperator"; a language, it was claimed, which would be "understood by all the competitors" (*The Times* July 14th 1908).

Once their majesties had settled into the box, the royal standard was run up by two bluejackets and the national anthem played. Lord Desborough stepped forward and requested His Majesty to open the Fourth Olympiad. The King in one ringing sentence declared "The Olympic Games of London are open," whereupon all the competitors and the spectators gave three hearty cheers.

The competing nations paraded with their standard bearers in alphabetical order. It was said to be a wonderful sight as the teams marched round the track. In total, there were some two thousand "young men and maidens, in the prime of life and the pink of condition" (*The Times* July 14th).

They were drawn up in a long line of fours. The French and the Germans found themselves marching together, which *The Times* hoped was "particularly well–omened in view of the deeper meaning of the Olympiad" (*The Times* July 14th).

The red and white stripes of the Austrian flag led the way with the Union Jack bringing up the rear. Some of the delegations dressed up for the event; the Swedes, Germans, Norwegians, Finns, Dutch and Italians were particularly impressive, and the Danish women in gymnastic costume "were most loudly and deservedly applauded" (Official Report).

The strong United States team were smartly dressed, although in their ordinary walking clothes, and said to have been "acclaimed with generous warmth by the whole gathering" (*Daily Telegraph* July 14th 1908).

The British team was led by an Oxford Blue and a Cambridge Blue, and a former member of the Eton Eight. The Russians made their first appearance at an Olympic Games with a team of just seven competitors.

Nonetheless, the parade fell well short of the spectacle now expected at modern Olympics and too many delegations simply paraded in plain clothes, or as in the case of the Australian swimming team, in their swimming gear and with bare feet.

The opening ceremony went down well with the spectators and overall was thought to have been a success. However, it had also marked the first disputes of the Games.

The Disputes Start

Even before the Games had started it was apparent that there were some political grievances and sensitivities which had the potential to cause problems. For a start, in 1908 there were tensions over the fact that Finland was under the political domination of Russia, and Ireland was still governed by Britain. In fact, the Games had begun badly for the Finns since they only just made the opening ceremony due to their boat being stranded off Hull with a defective boiler.

When they were refused permission by Russian officials to march under the Finnish flag, they decided to dispense with a standard bearer rather than march behind the flag of Czarist Russia, much to the displeasure of the Russian ambassador who was present. As for the Irish, they were outraged when they were informed that any of their athletic victories were to be counted as victories for Great Britain, and some of their most talented athletes withdrew rather than join the British team.

Those that did compete made a point of marching some distance behind the rest of the British team at the opening ceremony. Similarly, New Zealand had been granted dominion status in 1907 and it objected to having to compete with Australia as part of Australasia, whilst Austria, on the other hand, protested when Bohemia was allowed to enter a separate delegation.

But it was the incidents of the stadium flags which provoked the angriest reaction. When the United States and Swedish teams gathered for the march past they were shocked to discover that their national flags were missing from the brilliant forest of the flags of the competing nations that fluttered around the stadium. To make matters worse, the flags of China and Japan, who were not competing, were displayed! The Americans fumed and protested and the British explained that there had been an "administrative error",and they had been unable to find an American flag.

Since arrangements for the display of national flags had been left to the pro-American director of the Franco-British exhibition, Imre Kiralfy, it is hardly likely that he would have arranged for the Stars and Stripes not to be flown. But there were many Americans who suspected that the omission had been a deliberate slight, and during the opening parade several Americans made a point of carrying their own flags. The Swedes were equally furious, and when later they fell out with the British judges over the wrestling events, they withdrew from the Games. This proved embarrassing since the Swedes were hosting the next Olympics.

The trouble over the missing flags had barely subsided when another incident occurred which this time enraged British sensitivities. Arrangements had been made that as each delegation marched past the Royal Box their flags should be dipped in salute as a mark of respect to King Edward, who was also president of the British Olympic Association.

The Americans marched past led by their giant shot-putter, Ralph Rose, bearing what was now a particularly large and brilliant flag. To the displeasure of the King, Rose failed to dip the Stars and Stripes, and marched on. There were many Britons in the crowd who saw the incident as a deliberate slight to the monarch, and it helped precipitate some of the anti-American feeling amongst the spectators which later grew more pronounced. The Irish American Martin Sheridan is often alleged to have added fuel to the fire by making soon afterwards his famous remark that, "This flag dips to no earthly king". Whether in fact he did say that is somewhat doubtful (see chapter 13 on Ralph Rose). Nonetheless, wittingly or not, Rose had set a precedent, and to this day the Stars and Stripes is still not dipped to the head of state at Olympic parades.

Underway

With the parade over, the first event of the Games began with the heats of the 1500 metres and the Olympic record of 4 min 5.25 sec set at St Louis was soon broken despite the heavy condition of the track due to the rain. However, the stadium was by then far from full and only around one third of the seats around the ground were occupied.

The King himself stayed until 5.30pm and reportedly showed a keen interest in every detail of the afternoon's events, though he was said to be offended by the unruly behaviour of the American spectators.

Unfortunately, the flag incident, although somewhat trivial in itself, upset the American delegation and triggered their suspicions about the fairness of British officialdom. It did not help that the weather was miserable, and the team was so dissatisfied with their hotel in London that most of them decided to move to Brighton. From then onwards they were constantly complaining. In the first four days alone the Americans ominously lodged four official complaints.

Chapter 3

Trouble Ahead

"Oh, the British! They were out to get us, you know." – Johnny Hayes, winner of the London marathon.

The problems experienced before and during the opening ceremony showed that a more strident nationalistic note had entered into the spirit of the Games. It soon became apparent as competition commenced that the competing nations were very much aware that national prestige was at stake and were going to be critical of anything that hampered their chances of success. If the Games' organisers and officials thought that their troubles were over, they were to be sadly mistaken. The Olympic flame had been scarcely lit before a fresh round of disputes surfaced.

The decision to leave all the judging in the hands of Great Britain turned out to be a bad mistake. From the first day, many of the decisions of British judges and referees came under intense scrutiny by the national delegations, and none more so than by the American Olympic Committee who mounted a non-stop succession of protests. As the prominent American Olympic historian John Kieran noted,

"They also protested against the British attitude against American protests".

The British brought some of the problems on themselves by their insistence on administrative rules and procedures that annoyed other countries. For example, the drawing of the wrestling competition, the fact that too many events were scheduled to take place in the stadium at the same time, and the insistence that the American team were expected to wear knee-length running shorts. The American athletes subsequently wore theirs at mid-thigh length as a protest.

American officials also protested that no member of the American Olympic Committee was allowed on the stadium field during competition.

A more contentious issue was with the scoring system introduced by the British to decide the success of each nation, and more importantly which country was the overall champion. British officials scored the track and field events by awarding one point for each victory, and nothing for the second and third places.

Other countries, on the other hand, notably the Americans, advocated scoring also for second and third places. The sense of grievance was compounded by the fact that the events such as boxing, rowing, lacrosse and tennis were held outside the stadium, and were also to be scored. Since relatively few other countries participated in these events, the system was bound to put Great Britain well ahead of other nations. In the end the idea of a trophy for the overall championship winner was abandoned.

Similarly, there was criticism of the British system by which only the winners of the preliminary heats of the running events were allowed to go through to the next round. The Americans in particular soon became suspicious that their best athletes were deliberately being drawn together in the same heat. The matter came to a head when their two fastest middle distance runners had been forced to run against one another in the 1500 metres, and then again were drawn together in the 800 metres. It took an official protest for the organising committee to allow the two runners to compete separately in the latter race.

The bitter controversies which broke out in the following days on track and field arose undoubtedly from the rivalry between the British and American teams and some of the high-handed attitude and poor judgement of British officials. Each country wanted to prove that they were superior to the other. For the British competing on their home soil, their national pride was at stake. The American team came equally determined to win. High expectations of their success were whipped up by the media even before competition had started. The *New York Times* in successive headlines proclaimed that "American Athletes Sure of Success", "British Fear Yankee Athletes", and "We Will Knock The Spots Off The Britishers".

The intensity of the rivalry was heightened by

the presence of a relatively large number of Irish Americans in the United States team. Martin Sheridan, the American team captain and a member of the prestigious Irish American Club, pointed out that "Indeed if you were to go right through the team, the difficulty would be to pick out those who haven't at least some strain of Irish blood in them".

They relished the opportunity the 1908 Games provided to compete successfully against the best athletes in the world, and especially if they were from Great Britain. Several were sensitive to what they saw as Britain's denial of Irish independence, and they had no intention of ignoring any affront or to defer too readily to the imperial power. In addition, the Irish American Olympians were aware that the Games offered a good opportunity to help promote the Irish identity in America and to demonstrate their commitment and loyalty to their adopted country.

The Irish flavour of the team extended all the way to its officials and coaches. President Theodore Roosevelt had appointed John E Sullivan to lead the team. "Mike" Murphy, also of Irish descent, was appointed as the chief coach. Sullivan, the son of Irish immigrants, was the acknowledged Czar of American athletics. He was secretary to the powerful Amateur Athletic Union (AAU) and was said to hold the organised athletes of the American clubs in the hollow of his hand. He was a meticulous, no-nonsense organiser and publicist, but also a crusty, self-opinionated man who made more enemies than friends. He was once described by a compatriot as "a renegade Irishman, the purveyor of shameful and malicious falsehoods" (Mallon and Buchanan – *The 1908 Olympics Games*).

British officials at the London Games soon felt the same way, for Sullivan was a constant thorn in their sides. He came ready to criticise and with no intention of ever calming things down. Sullivan, along with other American officials, regarded the track and field events as America's athletics showpiece which reflected above all else the country's vitality. Soon after the Games started he said: "We have come here to win the championships in field sports and we are going to do it, despite the handicaps from which we are suffering" (*New York Daily Tribune* July 19th 1908).

As further disputes occurred, he lost no time in ensuring that many inflammatory and highly critical comments and articles on Britain's role in the Games were printed in the leading American newspapers.

In all, therefore, there was an inflammatory mixture in London already smouldering and waiting to burst into flames. There was not long to wait. The tug of war between teams from Great Britain and the United States was about to take place.

Chapter 4

Trouble Afoot

"The United States remained as competitors for the shortest time on record". (Daily Graphic).

On the fifth day of the Games the simmering animosity between Britain and America erupted into a real controversy in somewhat farcical circumstances. Fittingly, it occurred in the tug of war competition between the two countries. Only England, with three teams, and the Americans and Sweden with one team each, competed in the event. The row broke out over what the Americans considered to be illegal boots worn by the British team. The rules for the event used at the Games had been written by the British Olympic Association and specifically prohibited competitors from wearing "prepared boots or shoes with any projecting nails, tips, sprigs, points, hollows or projections of any kind".

The tug of war was a popular event in Britain and its teams had prepared themselves well for the Games. For the Americans, however, it was regarded as a minor event. Although their team was composed of some magnificent athletes, such as Ralph Rose, the shot putter, and John Flanagan, the hammer thrower, it was in effect a scratch team without any experience of how to tie an anchor or to place their men.

In the first round, they found themselves up against a British team composed of sturdy Liverpool policemen who wore heavy boots with metal rims, but no studs or other projections. To some American observers, however, their boots seemed so heavy that only with a great effort could the British team lift their feet from the ground! The American athletes, who wore just regulation shoes, took one look at the British team and protested about their boots. They were informed by the officials that the British boots were in fact acceptable since they were the standard police boots worn normally by the Liverpool team in their daily duties as "guardians of the King's peace and tranquility of the realm" (Kieran – *The Story of the Olympic Games*).

Although they were convinced that they were being unfairly treated, the Americans decided to compete. *The Sporting Life* reported that at the command, "heave", the Liverpool team of eight stalwart policemen "pulled the big men over the line like school boys, and the crowd collapsed with laughter". The Americans immediately lodged a formal protest on the grounds that the boots of the Liverpool team clearly gave them an unfair advantage.

The American coach, Matthew Halpin, told the event officials that if the rules were not adhered to, his team would not continue. The protest was disallowed, so the Americans walked off the field. Whereupon a British official lost no time in proclaiming that the Americans had retired, "because they had had enough of it" (*New York Times*).

When told of the incident Sullivan was furious. He was convinced that the British team were up to their tricks and had acted unfairly. It was the result, he accused, of "the work that dishonest officials did in committee rooms" (Mallon and Buchanan – *The 1908 Olympic Games*). A member of the American Committee even went to one of the largest shoe shops in London and asked to be shown a policeman's boot which, he claimed, turned out to be nothing like the ones the Liverpool policemen wore!

As an Olympic commissioner, and with the support of members of his tug of war team, Sullivan formally protested about the "prepared boots" of the Liverpool team to the British Olympic Association. The British Association promptly referred the case to the Amateur Athletic Association who ruled that the protest should be disallowed and confirmed that the British team were all policeman who had simply worn their ordinary duty boots. There were no prongs at the toes as the Americans alleged, and the boots could not be considered as specially prepared boots in any way.

The Times dismissed the fuss as "a mere affair of the moment". But the American delegation was thoroughly disgusted with what they felt to be a flagrantly unfair decision, which turned the American dressing room into what was called a camp of discontent. Predictably, James Sullivan soon ensured that their outrage was quickly reflected in the more sensational American press. Headlines in the *New York Times* proclaimed, "English Unfair in Olympic Games. US Protests against Holding the Tug-of-War. Complaint is Dismissed". And, "Liverpool Team Wears Monstrous Shoes That Arouse Ire of Americans Who Kick In Vain". Martin Sheridan also entered the fray through the column he wrote for the *New York Evening World* during the Olympics.

He commented that the American team had been handed a "real sour lemon" in the tug of war and that the Americans had gone into the event in regulation shoes without spikes, nails or tips, only to find the English team wearing shoes as big as "North River ferryboats". The Englishmen, he said, "had to waddle out on the field like a lot of County Mayo ganders going down to the public pond for a swim. The shoes they wore were the biggest things over here and were clearly made for the purpose of getting away with the event by hook as well as crook". In the final of the tug of war event, the Liverpool Police team was beaten by one from the London Police. This team afterwards challenged the Americans to a pull in their stockinged feet because they said, they did not wish the Americans to go back home dissatisfied with their beating and to give them the opportunity to show that they were as capable "tuggers" as they claimed to be.

Since the winning team of policemen had trained for the event for five months and "their condition was much admired", one can understand the reluctance of the American team to accept the challenge, and there is no record of it ever taking place.

Chapter 5

The Loneliness of a 400 metres runner

"These English officials will do anything to prevent an American or anybody besides their own people from winning a race." Mike Murphy – American coach.

At the start of the second week, the Games seemed to be settling down and for the previous few days had been mercifully free of any major disputes. And with the slight improvement in the weather and the lower entrance prices, the attendance at last began to pick up.

Britain was expected to do well in the finals of the track races, but in none more so than in the 400 metres which took place on Thursday July 23rd. The event had been built up by the British as the highlight of the Olympics as it featured the outstanding and hugely popular athlete, Lt Wyndham Halswelle. In the event, the race was run in highly controversial and dramatic circumstances, and unleashed a storm of protest shattering completely the relative calm of the preceding few days.

Aged 26, Halswelle was a London-born Scot, a Boer War veteran, and a holder of several middle distance records. In the final of the 400 metres he was joined by three Americans – the black runner John Taylor of the Irish American club, WC Robbins of Harvard and JC Carpenter of Cornell. Another American, Paul Pilgrim, who had won the 400 metres and 800 metres gold medals at the 1906 Olympics, had already been eliminated.

Halswelle, the AAA champion, had set the fastest time in the preliminary rounds when he ran a new Olympic record of 48.4 seconds. He was the clear favourite. But the crowd, mostly British, were tense and apprehensive.

There were no lanes in the final and newspaper stories all over England carried rumours that the "Yankee gang" were going to use team tactics to thwart Halswelle. The more sensational papers predicted that Halswelle could expect trouble and urged spectators to bear in mind that, in an emergency, the old instructions issued by Lord Nelson at Trafalgar were in force: that England expected every man to do his duty. Needless to say the American contingent saw this as little more than incitement to riot (Webster – *Olympic Cavalcade*).

The British officials, too, were nervous and had stationed officials every twenty yards around the track. The veteran American coach, "Mike" Murphy, warned his three finalists of the feeling around the stadium and urged them to keep out of trouble. They promised to do so. The starter, Harry Gable, made a point too of warning the runners against any wilful jostling during the race, which, he said, would be re-run if that were the case and the offender disqualified.

Taylor got off to a poor start and was never in contention. John Carpenter, who was a full second slower than Halswelle at his best, took the lead from the start followed by Robbins and Halswelle. Carpenter set off at world record pace and had opened up a twelve metre lead at the halfway point. The crowd was in a frenzy, and urged Halswelle to close the gap. As the athletes approached the final turn of the track with one hundred yards to go, Carpenter, Robbins and Halswelle were closely bunched and fighting for the lead.

The following day *The Times* gave this account of the race: "The Americans were leading with the Englishman (sic) Halswelle third. Halswelle closed until almost even when the American who was next to him began to run wide, with the result that soon after Halswelle turned the bend he was forced very nearly on to the bicycle track.

"The interference with Halswelle appeared to the judges so palpable that they broke the tape while the race was still in progress before the runners reached the winning post. It certainly seemed as if the Americans had run the race on a definite and carefully thought-out plan. It was not as if Carpenter, the one who forced Halswelle to run wide and elbowed him severely as he tried to pass him, had himself taken a wide curve at the bend and then run straight on.

"He appeared rather to run diagonally, crossing in front of the Englishman so that he was obliged to lose several yards. That is a fair and impartial account of what happened as far as it could be judged from the stand."

Not surprisingly, the Americans were to see the incident at the turn quite differently. It was claimed that with "characteristic dumbness", Halswelle had tried to pass Carpenter on the outside and at no time did Carpenter foul the British runner. In fact, it was said Carpenter was at the turn of the bend already pulling away from Halswelle who "was stale from his unnecessarily and foolishly fast trials of two days before, and the fast 300 yards had killed him off" (Whitney – *Outing* magazine).

Even before the end of the race there was mayhem. British officials ran on to the track, shouting to the crowd and to the chief judge: "Foul work on the part of the Americans" and "No race." A British official, a Scot, made sure that the winning tape was cut and held up his hand before either of the two leading Americans could reach it. The American runner Taylor was pulled off the track by officials. For a moment the American athletes and their officials were left stunned by the events they had just witnessed but then they surrounded the British officials, shouting their protests. A howl went up from the crowd: "Disqualify the dirty runner," and thereupon spectators left their seats and poured on to the field. In the pandemonium that followed British and American spectators argued and yelled abuse at one another. It took a full half an hour before the track could be cleared by several sturdy London policemen who were called in to restore order.

An hour-long debate raged before the British judges declared the race void and informed spectators that the race would be re-run on the following Saturday, the last day of the competition. Carpenter walked off disconsolately, and in disgust. The American officials were outraged and immediately lodged an official protest. The committee of the AAA was called upon to reconsider the judges' decision. Much to the Americans' disquiet, the committee called only Halswelle and the judges to the hearing – no American testimony was requested or given – and finally decided Carpenter had to be disqualified, and that just Halswelle, Taylor and Robbins should re-run the race two days later.

The American team leader, Sullivan, and the coach, Murphy, were furious. "Never in my life," said Sullivan, "and I have been attending athletic meetings for thirty-one years, have I witnessed a scene that struck me as being so unsportsmanlike and unfair" (Schaap – *An Illustrated History of the Olympics*).

The members of the American Olympic Committee, said the *New York Times*, were so outraged as to become "the most disgusted lot of Americans ever gathered together in England". John Keiran declared that "if there had been a boat leaving Shepherd's Bush that night for New York, the United States athletes and officials probably would have torn down what they could of the stadium and then rushed up the gang-plank for home" (Keiran – *The Story of the Olympic Games*).

Taylor and Robbins were told to boycott the re-running of the race. Robbins waited until the following day before reaching a decision that he would not run in protest against the actions of the British officials.

He placed no personal pressure on Taylor to follow his example. It is probable that Taylor would have dearly liked to have had the opportunity to be the first black athlete to win an Olympic gold medal, but he too decided to withdraw in support of his colleagues. (Taylor in fact later did win his gold medal as part of the gold medal-winning American team in the medley relay.)

In the uncontested re-run, Halswelle circled the track in a time of 50.0 seconds. He did so "with great personal dignity", and his run was accompanied, said the *Glasgow Herald*, by "continuous cheering". His victory represents the only walkover in Olympic history. He became the first Scot to win an Olympic gold medal. There is no record that Carpenter ever again competed in an official 400 metres race.

It is interesting to compare the two athletes' versions of the event. Halswelle maintained that he did not attempt to pass Carpenter until the last corner so as to reserve his effort for the finishing straight. Here, he "attempted to pass Carpenter on the outside, since he was not far enough from the curb to do so on the inside, and I was too close to have crossed behind him.

"Carpenter's elbow undoubtedly touched my chest, for as I moved outwards to pass him he did likewise, keeping his right (side) in front of me. In this manner he bored me across quite two thirds of the track, and entirely stopped my running. As I was well up to his shoulder, and endeavouring to pass him, it is absurd to say that I could have come up on the inside" (*The Sporting Life*).

On the other hand, Carpenter, in his version of events, maintained that at the final bend he and Halswelle were running absolutely abreast of one another, "with plenty of room on the outside of him, and he could have passed me on the inside of me if necessary. I do not know of any contact between us at any point during the race. I do not know how a race could have been more fairly run. We raced him off his feet. He couldn't stand the pace" (*Daily Mail*, July 24th 1908).

The Times did its best to calm the storm by expressing the hope that "both countries will agree to say as little as possible about this most unfortunate incident which no one can regret more than the English".

But too much ill feeling had been aroused and the recriminations continued. The *Daily News* described the incident as distinctly unsavoury. The conservative London journal, *The Sportsman*, did not mince its words, calling the race "one of the most disgraceful exhibitions of foul play ever witnessed. A slur is cast upon American sportsmanship in the eyes of all Europe which cannot ever be eradicated. There can be no excuse; the thing was open, unabashed and shameless" (Schaap – *Illustrated History of the Olympics*).

As far as the Americans were concerned, it confirmed their worst fears that there was a British conspiracy against their athletes. The events of the previous week, hostile spectators, and the unsporting habit of the British judges using their megaphones to urge on the British competitors, had done little for the British reputation for fairness and impartiality.

The *New York Herald* proclaimed that, "In the opinion of Americans who saw the Olympic Games to-day the last nail was driven into the coffin of the putrescent thing that has been paraded before the eyes of the world as 'British fair play'."

The American coach, Murphy, made sure that the controversy lived on in the British and American newspapers for several months. He told the *Daily Tribune*, "highway robbery is pretty strong language, but there are no other words for it. I have been up against the English officials for years, and it has always been the same story – they would have robbed us of everything they could". To the *American Evening Post* he stated that "It shows what the boasted fairest sportsman in the world will do to win ... and, if I had my way, every American athlete at the stadium would leave here right away, and never return, either to this arena or to England".

And the athlete John Taylor on his return home also made public his disgust at the British actions by declaring to reporters, "to deal with those Englishmen gave us about the worst thing I ever heard of. It was simply a plain piece of robbery. That 400 metre race should have gone to the credit of America and not England (sic) is the unanimous opinion of the Americans and is shared by not a few Englishmen. Just think of them deliberately pulling me off the track and not allowing me to finish" (Henry Chase – *American Visions*).

Part of the trouble was due to the fact that the race was run without proper lanes and with four fast runners would inevitably be very physical. Nor did it help that the racing rules between Britain and the United States at that time differed with the Americans having a more relaxed view about interference during the race. This was an anomaly that the international bodies later removed in the light of the 1908 race.

Subsequently, athletics specialists have reviewed the evidence, and the general opinion is that the photographs do show that Carpenter had indeed, intentionally or not, run wide and badly impeded Halswelle's course. Since the race was being run in England where the rules prohibited any form of obstruction, it therefore seemed reasonable for the appeal committee to punish the offender and to order a re-run.

Even if there is still a doubt about the legality of Carpenter's disqualification, his running was certainly unsportsmanlike, and could not be excused. On the other hand, most authorities also agree that the behaviour of the British officials during and after the event was arbitrary and over-officious, and intensified greatly the American anger as to how the Games were being run.

In retrospect, however, the controversy did lead to one beneficial outcome. After the 1908 Games the supervision and judging of all events was removed from the host country and placed with international groups.

In August 1908, *The Scotsman* reported that a match had been arranged for a Scottish team to compete against the Irish American club which would have brought Halswelle and Carpenter together again, but the match never took place.

Chapter 6

Marathon Drama

"The problem was that people along the pavement were giving him glasses of brandy instead of water. Pietri wasn't exhausted, he was drunk." – Joe Deakin, British athlete.

The marathon that took place on the afternoon of Friday July 24th 1908 is probably the most famous and dramatic event in Olympic history. It will always be remembered as Dorando Pietri's marathon. The little Italian from the small town of Carpi, near Reggio, won the hearts of the nation and world fame, but was denied a gold medal.

At last the rain had stopped and the day of the race dawned fine. By the afternoon it had become exceptionally hot and humid; ideal, said *The Times*, "for a bathe or game of cricket perhaps, but terrible for a feat of endurance of mind, stamina, muscle, and feet". The temperature eventually reached 78° F (26 C), and the road authorities in every town and village along the route had arranged to sprinkle the roads to keep them as cool and dust free as possible. However, the AAA made no concession as regards the athletes' so-called costume, insisting that

"Every competitor must wear complete clothing from the shoulder to the knees. Any competitor will be excluded from taking part in the race unless properly attired".

The runners and their attendants may have drawn some comfort from the fact that accommodation was available for a wash at several hotels along the route. The Oxo company, the chief caterers, also supplied refreshments free of charge to the competitors. These included hot and cold Oxo, rice pudding, raisins, bananas, soda and milk. Runners were warned at the start of the race not to take any drug or they would be disqualified. No mention was made of the copious quantities of beer, champagne and spirits that were to be made freely available from spectators lining the route.

The race started on the East Terrace of Windsor Castle, some seven hundred yards from Queen Victoria's statue. The route went through Slough, Uxbridge, Ruislip, Harrow, Willesden, Harlesden, and across Wormwood Scrubs, where the prisoners lined the walls and cell windows to watch the event and on to the White City. By far the most punishing part of the course was over the last four miles. *The Times* reported that the finish was exceptionally severe for such a long race and the men who succeeded in reaching the stadium "will in all probability have performed a feat which for combined speed and endurance is unparalleled in the annals of running".

The total distance of the race was 26 miles 385

yards. It is generally assumed that this precise distance arose out of the wishes of members of the British royal family to have the race start near the castle so it could be witnessed by them, and then to have the finish line directly opposite the Royal Box. In a carefully researched article for the magazine *Track Stats*, Hugh Farey has thrown doubt on both these assumptions. He has pointed out that the distance of the race was in fact set by the trial marathon organised by the Polytechnic Harriers shortly before the Olympics, and that the finish was more to do with the complexities of the Franco-British Exhibition than the wishes of the royal family.

No doubt inspired to some extent by the heroic legend of Pheidippides in the ancient Olympics, marathon running had become a very popular event since the Games had been restored in 1896. The London Games were no exception and the race gripped the imagination and interest of the nation. It was estimated that a quarter of a million people lined the route, and a huge crowd of ninety thousand had gathered in the White City Stadium. As *The Sporting Life* summed up the excitement, "The country that wins the marathon need not do anything else for glory".

Fifty-five competitors from sixteen nations lined up for the start. The favourite was the American, Thomas Morrissey, who had won the Boston Marathon earlier in the year. Britain had some good marathon runners and fielded a strong team.

The newspaper, *The People*, left its readers in no doubt that "it will be a keen disappointment if the marathon race falls to a foreign competitor, because that event, above all others, should give proof that our native pluck and grit are not extinct".

Even the disgruntled American team manager, James Sullivan, predicted that Great Britain would win the race. The Canadians also fielded a strong twelve-man team including the outstanding Canadian/Indian runner, Tom Longboat, who boasted before the race that any athlete that beat him "will have to go". Pietri, aged 23, and the American, Johnny Hayes, 22, also had good records in their own countries but were regarded as outsiders.

At about 2.30pm at a signal from the Princess of Wales, Lord Desborough fired the starting gun, and despite the burning sun the runners dashed off "at a lively pace" for the gates leading into the town.

By the ten mile mark, two British runners, Fred Price and Jack Lord, led by fifty yards from Charles Hefferon, a South African but British by birth, and Pietri. At the halfway mark at Ruislip, Price led the race by two hundred yards but shortly afterwards the British runners wilted and Hefferon went to the front. A challenge was made by Longboat, but he too fell back and eventually collapsed and retired. The American runners were calmly and sensibly running their own race and made no attempt to force the pace.

At eighteen miles the race seemed to lie between Hefferon and Pietri, with the former still leading by more than three minutes. However, two miles from the stadium the South African made a bad mistake. Virtually exhausted, he accepted a glass of champagne from a spectator and within a mile he developed stomach cramps and became dizzy. Pietri saw his opportunity and urged on by the spectators overtook Hefferon. But the effort took a lot out of him and Johnny Hayes, after overtaking Hefferon, was soon closing fast on Pietri.

Meanwhile, the spectators crammed into the stadium had been kept informed of the positions of the leading runners by a huge placard paraded around the field and had picked up that Hayes was in third place at twenty miles. However, thereafter the position of the American went missing. The last report spectators received was that South Africa and Italy were in the lead, and the assumption of many spectators was that Hayes must have dropped out.

In the stadium the pent-up excitement of the huge crowd intensified as the runners drew nearer. Interest in the pole vault and wrestling lingered and then died.

The divers left their diving stage, wrapped themselves in their dressing gowns, and settled on the grass. Officials, policemen and photographers took their positions, the band ceased playing and all eyes were fixed on the entrance to the stadium (*Manchester Guardian*, July 25th 1908).

Some two hundred yards before entering the stadium, Pietri fell exhausted. It is not clear what happened next, but some accounts say that at this point he was examined by a physician and given a hypodermic of strychnine, a common stimulant in use at the time. [At the St Louis Games of 1904, Thomas Hicks, the marathon winner, was said to have received small doses of strychnine from his trainers and ran "the last ten miles in something of a mental haze" (Kieran – *The Story of the Olympic Games)*.].

If so, that would have been enough to disqualify Pietri automatically. He was assisted to his feet and tried to run on. In the stadium, the spectators were told by megaphone – "The runners are coming" – and all eyes were fixed on the entrance as the little Italian staggered in.

He made a most distressing sight. There, said *The Times* correspondent, "a tired man, dazed, bewildered, hardly conscious, in red shorts and white vest, his hair white with dust staggers on to the track... He looks about him, hardly knowing where he is. Just the knowledge that somehow, by some desperate resolve of determination, he must get round the 200 yards to the tape of the finish keeps him on his feet".

The crowd tried to rally him with their cheers, all regard for nationality forgotten. They gasped when Pietri headed off in the wrong direction. Officials rushed forward and he was suddenly engulfed by "30 enthusiastic partisans".

They pointed him to the right way but within a few yards he collapsed on the track. The slope of the archway into the stadium had apparently been the final straw. Most of the crowd knew little or nothing about the Italian but by now they were emotionally behind him. Some screamed for the officials to help him, while others, knowing that any assistance would automatically disqualify him, called out to leave him alone.

At first the officials let Pietri struggle on, but in the words of the official report, "It was impossible to leave him there, for it looked as if he might die in the very presence of the Queen." Four times within the stadium he fell, and four times British officials and doctors rushed to help him get to his feet and to plod on. He fell again just thirty yards from the finish and lay lifeless on the track.

The author Arthur Conan Doyle wrote that: "He was in a few yards of my seat. Amid stooping figures and grasping hands I caught a glimpse of the haggard, yellow face, the glazed, expressionless eyes, the lank, black hair streaked across the brow. Surely he is done now. He cannot rise again". From the Royal Box the Queen watched the Italian's brave attempts to struggle on, "With tender, womanly sympathy – and tears which she did not try to hide, were in her eyes" (*The Sporting Life*).

At this moment another runner entered the stadium. To the shock and horror of the British spectators, it was not Hefferon, "a good man of the Empire", but the Irish American, Johnny Hayes.

Relatively fresh, he ran steadily round the track and in a minute would have passed the helpless Italian. The crowd yelled, "Dorando! Dorando! Come on! He's got you! He's got you!"

It was all too much for the British officials. The clerk of the course, JM Andrews, and the medical attendant Dr MJ Bulger picked up Pietri and frog-marched him across the line, thereby creating the most famous image in Olympic history.

Despite the clear violation of the rules which had just taken place, the judges announced Pietri as the winner, and the Italian flag was immediately run up the victory pole. Some two hours after the official United States protest, the British reversed the decision: Pietri was disqualified and Hayes declared the winner.

The action taken by the British officials, and the long time it took them to uphold the United States protest, greatly angered the Americans. It was another huge blow to their already strained relations, and obscured the fact that their runners had done very well. Despite Sullivan's prediction, there were four Americans placed in the top ten of the race, and the first English runner had finished only twelfth, and eight others had dropped out.

Hayes had actually completed the course some twenty minutes faster than the first British runner. It was a humiliation for a country that considered itself the home of the long distance runner. Many Englishman felt bitter about the manner of Hayes' victory and thought the Americans had somehow acted unsportingly. A rumour was even spread that some British officials had somehow obtained a photograph of Hayes being carried along the marathon course in a blanket!

As for Pietri, he was taken from the stadium to hospital on a stretcher. His heart was said to have been displaced by half an inch and he was said to have spent some time near to death following the race. In fact the agency, *Central News*, stunned everybody by putting out a brief message – "Dorando is dead".

Happily, his recovery seems to have been remarkable. At 9pm he was sufficiently recovered from his ordeal to walk to a taxi cab and drive to his apartment. The next day he was complaining that the British officials should have left him alone, and, "if the doctor had not ordered the attendants to pick me up, I believe I could have finished unaided" (Schaab – *An Illustrated History of the Olympics*).

Overnight Pietri became an international celebrity, the first sporting superstar. In unofficial terms he was treated as the winner. At the closing ceremony on July 25th Queen Alexandra further annoyed the Americans by paying special attention to him. She presented him personally with a gold cup which was the exact replica of the one awarded to the winner, Johnny Hayes.

Since there was no time to get Pietri's cup engraved, the Queen also gave him an accompanying card with the words: "For P. Dorando, In Remembrance of the Marathon race from Windsor to the stadium, From Queen Alexandra".

Pietri later exhibited the cup at the Hammersmith Palais and other venues. Irving Berlin composed his famous tune, "Pietri", in his honour, and Conan-Doyle declared that: "No Roman prince ever has borne himself better; the great breed is not yet extinct".

His effigy appeared in Madame Tussaud's museum. On the other side of the Atlantic, President Theodore Roosevelt's initial reaction to Hayes' victory was more modest: "I am so glad," he said, "that a New York boy won it".

The Dorando Pietri affair was not the only protest from the Americans about the marathon. Even before the race had started, the United States had made at least three protests to the British Olympic Committee about the participation of Longboat in the event, claiming that he was a professional. As the account of Longboat's life in Chapter 15 shows, the protest was not without some justification, but since the Canadian Olympic Committee had investigated the matter and concluded there was no firm evidence, the BOC turned down the protest.

Arguably, the event could also have given rise to another protest, this time involving Hefferon, who was awarded the silver medal after Pietri's disqualification. Some of his supporters wanted him to protest that Hayes had arrived at the stadium nearly as exhausted as Pietri, and alleged the American also had been given assistance by some compatriots on the track. Hefferon would have none of it, saying, "I would rather not win such a race at all than win on a protest" (Webster – *Olympic Cavalcade*).

Another interesting aspect of the marathon relates to the involvement of Sir Arthur Conan Doyle. Best remembered as the creator of the famous detective, Sherlock Holmes, his part in the final dramatic scenes in the stadium is much less well-known. Conan Doyle was in fact at the side of the track in his dual capacity as a correspondent for the *Daily Mail*, and as the marathon medical officer. He was one of the officials who have been identified as giving Pietri some assistance on the track. Conan Doyle always maintained that Pietri's disqualification was unjust since the runner had not asked for assistance. Perhaps he felt some guilt himself for the incident, for it was at his instigation that the *Daily Mail* mounted a public subscription for Pietri to buy a bakery in his home town.

Chapter 7

2,000 men – 36 women

"In the games in London were assembled some two thousand young men (and 36 women), the athletic representatives of their various races, who met each other inspired by the same ideals of physical excellence, and competed with each other in friendly rivalry."
– BOA Official Report on the 1908 Games.

It is easy to let the achievements of the 1908 Games become overshadowed by the controversies that took place. The fact remains that London staged an international sporting contest far exceeding anything organised or seen ever before. The standard of performance over the greatly expanded programme of different sports was generally very high. There were many outstanding and memorable achievements and several new Olympic and world records were set.

The sprint races – 100 and 200 metres – were very popular. The Americans had dominated the events in the past Olympics, and it was a big disappointment to them when two athletes from the British Empire managed to break their monopoly.

In the 100 metres race, the American, Jimmy Rector, was a hot favourite having tied the Olympic record of 10.8 seconds in the semi-finals. In a closely fought final, however, he was beaten by a relatively unknown nineteen-year-old clerk from South Africa, Reggie Walker.

Apparently Walker, although finishing only second in the AAA championships shortly before the Olympics, had caught the eye of the famous London-born coach, Sam Mussabini. He spent the next few weeks improving Walker's running, especially his start, and the coaching paid off brilliantly when Walker won the final by a good yard.

The South African became an instant hero and the partisan British crowd of nearly fifty thousand erupted with a tremendous cheer and threw their hats into the air. As one American newspaper put it, they were overjoyed to see "the monotonous succession of American victories broken by a Briton, even if he was a colonist".(Wallechinsky – *The Complete Book of the Olympics*).

The bashful Walker was overwhelmed as friends and officials competed for the honour of carrying him off the field in triumph whilst the stadium bands played exultantly.

Mussabini had another more famous Olympic success some years later when he coached Harold Abrahams to his 100 metres victory at the Paris Olympics in 1924.

A further shock came in the 200 metres when

the Irish Canadian sprinter, Bobby Kerr, beat two strong Americans by just one foot in a very closely-fought race. As a teenager, Kerr had joined the International Harvester Fire Brigade, whose employees were renowned for their speed of foot. He allegedly found training exhausting and reckoned to run his best only when he had dined and wined well. It is said that he made sure he was out on the town until the early hours of the morning before the Olympic final. Kerr later captained the 1924 Canadian Olympic team.

Despite these disappointments and the disastrous 400 metres final, the Americans had their revenge in the 800 and 1500 metres races. The heats for the latter event were run in the first week of the Games and five of the eight finalists were British, including the favourites, Harold Wilson and Norman Hallows. Mel Sheppard, a shy New Yorker, was one of the two American qualifiers who, it was said, only ran best when he was angry. The story has it that his shrewd American coach made sure he went into the race in the right frame of mind by telling him shortly beforehand, in front of other American athletes, that he had no chance of winning. In a brilliant sprint finish, the enraged Sheppard beat Wilson in a new Olympic record time.

In the following week Sheppard followed up his success by winning the 800 metres by the convincing margin of ten yards, and set a new world record. In addition, he went on to win his third gold medal of the Games as a member of the victorious American medley relay team.

The United States dominated the hurdle races. The four finalists in the 110 metres hurdles were all Americans, yet prior to the race they had not competed against one another before. Although he had never before run as fast as his rivals, Forrest Smithson won the race in 15 seconds, a world and Olympic record. As a theology student he had protested against the decision to run the final on a Sunday and a legend grew that he ran the race carrying a Bible in his left hand! Attractive as it might sound, there is no real evidence to support this story. Equally impressive was the victory of his compatriot, Charles Bacon, in the 400 metres hurdles which he won in 55 seconds, again another world record.

American athletes also did well in the stadium field events. Ray Ewry was the best standing jumper in the world. At the Paris Games he had been dubbed "The Human Frog" after his incredible leaping ability. By winning the standing high jump and the standing long jump in London (both events are now defunct), he brought his tally of official gold medals to ten over the four Olympiads in which he had competed. No one in Olympic history has ever exceeded this number of individual gold medals. His achievements are even more remarkable since he had once been an invalid. He had contracted polio as a boy and had taken up athletics in order to build up the strength of his legs.

Martin Sheridan, the outstanding Irish American athlete, won both the freestyle and Greek style discus competitions, which gave him a remarkable career total of five gold medals. And in wet and slippery conditions, the giant American, Ralph Rose, won the second of his gold medals in the shot-put. (More about the lives of these two all time greats in Olympic history can be found later in this book.) To complete a clean sweep for the Americans in the throwing events, John Flanagan, a thirty-six-year-old Irishman representing the United States, won the hammer event with his last throw by beating the world record holder, Matt McGrath, another American.

Problems arose in the pole vault competition. Traditionally, vaulters had used a pole with a spike on the bottom and planted it into the ground to start their upward launch. But by 1908 a new technique, which is now standard, had been developed whereby the vaulters planted their non-spiked poles into a hole dug at the running end. The British officials refused to allow this method to be used, and the American competitors, much to their annoyance, were forced to change their poles. The vaulters also complained about the lack of a sandpit or bales of straw to break their falls. And to make matters worse the competition was delayed considerably by the dramatic scenes at the end of the marathon. Finally, when the Americans Edward Cooke and Alfred Gilbert tied for first place, it was decided that a jump-off would not be appropriate and each should be awarded a gold medal.

Leaving aside the tug of war, the only field events not won by an American were the javelin, which was won by the Swede, Eric Lemming, and the triple jump, won by the Irish athlete, Tim Ahearne, who competed for Great Britain. The javelin, in fact, provided the spectators with some excitement otherwise lacking on a dull day of competition. A plentiful supply of javelins were placed on the field and, since there was no definite order of throwing, the flights of several implements whirling through the air was quite thrilling at times. The British competitors, the *Manchester Guardian* reported, knew nothing about how to throw the javelin and it was kindest to be silent as to their names and performances!

In the walking events, George Larner, of Great Britain, completed a double by winning both the 3500 metres and 10 mile races, setting a new world record for the latter. As a policeman he was reputed to have perfected his heel and toe technique on his beat, which included patrolling the beach at Brighton. He had some interesting views on training, advising that: "When circumstances permit all clothing should be removed for a run round a secluded garden, especially if it is raining at the time" (Wallechinsky – *Complete Book of the Olympics*).

Away from the track and field, Great Britain, with its strong competitive tradition in many different sports, was easily the most successful nation. Many sports were held at venues away from the White City and had attracted comparatively few foreign competitors. The British won every gold medal in the rowing, boxing, sailing and the men's and women's tennis, and also won the competitions in polo, water polo, hockey and soccer.

In the boxing, Dick Gunn, at the age of thirty-eight, achieved the distinction of being the oldest fighter ever to win an Olympic boxing title when he won at featherweight. Gunn had to be coaxed out of retirement for the Olympics after an eight-year lay-off. He had been ABA champion from 1894–1896 and had retired at the request of the boxing authorities because of "his acknowledged superiority over all-comers".

He had lost only once in fifteen years. Another British boxing victory worthy of note was in the middleweight division. Johnny Douglas became the only man to have played in Test cricket and to win an Olympic gold when he narrowly beat the Australian, Reginald "Snowy" Baker in a fierce contest. Baker went on to win fame and fortune in other fields (see Chapter 18).

The swimming programme was far superior to anything before seen at an Olympics. It consisted of six races, two diving competitions and water polo, all conducted in the specially constructed swimming pool in the middle of the stadium. Henry Taylor, at the age of twenty-three, became the most successful swimmer Britain has ever produced when he won gold medals in the 400 metres and 1500 metres freestyle. He also anchored the successful British 800 metre relay team by overtaking the great Hungarian swimmer, Zoltan von Halmay, on the last length in dramatic circumstances (see Chapter 16).

The London Games saw the first proper international football tournament held at the Olympics. The Games of 1900, 1904, and 1906 had included demonstration events but they had been contested only by clubs and scratch teams and were not considered official competitions. Eight national teams entered in London (including two from France) but Hungary and Bohemia withdrew before the start because of political trouble in the Balkans.

The Football Association organised the event and entered a "Great Britain" team which was in fact the England national amateur team. Several members of the team played with professional clubs, notably the England captain, Vivian Woodward, who played for Tottenham Hotspur. Another member of the team, Harold Hardman, later became the chairman of Manchester United.

In a closely fought final, Great Britain beat Denmark by two goals to nil. Most observers were disappointed at the performance of the British team whose forwards were particularly disappointing, whereas the Danes "played throughout with splendid pluck and dash." (*Observer* October 25th 1908) In an earlier match against France "A" the Danish centre forward, Sven Nielson, had scored ten goals, an Olympic record that stood for more than ninety years.

The ice skating events were staged at Prince's Skating Rink in Knightsbridge in October. The event is particularly significant for three reasons. First, it was the first time that a winter sport such as figure skating had been staged at an Olympic Games.

Secondly, women were allowed to compete for the first time and the British skater Madge Syers, at the age of twenty-seven, became the first Olympics ladies' figure skating gold medallist.

Syers was the pioneer of women's figure skating and her life and achievements are described in Chapter 17. Thirdly, the event provided the small Russian team with their first Olympic gold medal when Nikolai Panin defeated two British entries in the Special Figures.

Regarding some of the other competitions, the cycling was badly affected by the poor July weather which flooded the track on several occasions. Five out of the six events were won by British riders. In the archery, William Dodd of Great Britain took the gold. Brought up in a very wealthy family, and well accustomed to a life of exceptional leisure, he enlisted at the age of forty-seven as an army private in World War I.

Finding life in the trenches far from his liking, he rapidly engineered a transfer to the navy where he served in an administrative job. When his sister, Lottie, finished second in the women's archery event, they became the first brother and sister medallists in Olympic history. Lottie was also the youngest winner of the Wimbledon tennis championships, winning the title five times.

Finally, a number of demonstration events were held alongside the competitive events, which the organisers considered merited inclusion in future Games. Some, such as the bicycle polo, in which an Irish team beat a German one by 3-1, remained one-off occasions, but others were eventually to take a full place in the Olympic programme. Perhaps the most important was women's gymnastics. The display by women from Scandinavia was warmly applauded with "the Danish girls' splendid form being generally admired" (*The Scotsman* July 13th 1908).

It was, however, not until Amsterdam and the 1928 Games that a medal event for women's gymnastics was held.

Chapter 8

America fumes, Britain blusters

"Hurrah for old England, the seat of the Fourth Olympiad, the land of sport and fair play!"
– Count Brunetta D'Usseaux – speaking for the IOC at the closing banquet.

The summer Olympic Games were brought to a close on Saturday July 25th. Finals of several events were held in the morning. Apart from the sad sight of Wyndham Halswelle having to complete an uncontested run to achieve his hollow victory in the 400 metres, the remaining events were mercifully free of controversy. As the athletes departed for their homes, it was time to take stock of how the Games had gone.

The American team had good reason to celebrate. They had done very well in the track and field and they returned to much rejoicing in the United States. The *New York Herald* proudly proclaimed that the American triumph in the Marathon amounted to the "victorious scream of the American eagle, and it smote the ears of the confident prophets of British success". The president, Theodore Roosevelt, greeted the team at his summer home in Oyster Bay, and on behalf of the nation congratulated them on their success. He greatly admired most forms of physical exertion, and is said to have exclaimed, "By George, I'm so glad to see all you boys!" (*New York Times*). In New York a massive celebration was held. It was, said the *New York Times*, "the greatest ovation in the history of athletics" and one which celebrated those, "brawny representatives of young America (who) faced the multitudes in the London Stadium perfectly unconcerned and won the most glorious victory in the annals of athletics".

Twenty thousand people marched in a parade through the city with the returning athletes, and many thousands more lined the streets which were decorated with American flags. The athletes were each given gold cups, and speeches were made praising their victories in spite of what was claimed to be the efforts of the perfidious British.

As for Great Britain, there were no similar national celebrations but plenty of satisfaction that overall the British competitors had acquitted themselves well. In official circles the reaction to the Games was, initially at least, cool and measured. The organisers were pleased that the great majority of the competing nations had returned home openly praising the arrangements made for the Games and the fair play and hospitality shown to them.

At an official banquet after the Olympics, organised by the BOC for officials and competitors, Lord Desborough was warmly cheered when he spoke of how the Games had brought together a trained body of athletes from nearly every civilised country who had competed amicably in the finest arena ever constructed for the purpose. And true to the Olympic ideals, his audience applauded his view that as long as the competing nations departed as friends there remained no reason why the Games should not make an important contribution to international harmony and understanding. Significantly, however, the United States was not one of the nations represented at the banquet.

The Times agreed that the Games had provided some wonderful feats of athletic endurance and skill. But at the same time it acknowledged that it had not all been plain sailing, and that "the perfect harmony which every one wished for has been marred by certain regrettable disputes and protests to the judges' rulings."

It regretted that in many newspapers the whole world over, national feeling had run riot. The newspaper also admitted that in all honesty the stadium events had shown that: "We have learned some useful lessons ... in speed and strength we are far behind the Americans ... When we analyse the results of the strictly athletic contests our national pride receives a severe blow".

However, there were others in Britain who were inclined to be far less charitable towards the United States and made their criticisms known through the press. Some plainly resented the American success, and others condemned the brashness and unsporting behaviour of the American team and their supporters.

"The only unpleasant feature of the Games", declared the English Magazine, *Academy*, "has been the unseemly behaviour of the American contingent, who had sat in great masses emitting disgusting noises and cries". And as for the 400 metres dispute, *Academy* protested that "A more disgraceful exhibition of foul running has never been seen on an English track, and it is becoming increasingly obvious that in future American 'Amateurs' will have to be debarred from taking part in athletic contests in this country, which are supposed to be reserved for gentlemen".

The *Morning Advertiser* pondered over why present day Americans were such bad sportsmen. The trouble was, it concluded, "that they are a young nation and they will require a good many years' training in sport before they can attain to our level".

Back in the United States any hopes that the Games' controversies would soon be forgotten as tempers cooled were quickly dashed. Far too much antagonism towards the "foul tactics" of the British officials and their high-handed manner had been whipped up by the sensational press for this to happen.

Opinion became openly critical and pessimistic about the future of the Olympics. Leading American sporting officials and opinion formers, and above all James Sullivan, were particularly embittered about their experience in London, claiming they had been cheated, and convinced that radical changes were needed if the Olympic movement was to have any future at all.

Consequently, on both sides of the Atlantic a veritable war of words broke out as protagonists used the press and other means to voice their comments and criticisms of one another. The *New York Times* wasted no time in declaring that the Olympiad, "while an athletic success, as a means of promoting international friendship has been a deplorable failure". The newspaper claimed that the relationships between English and American officials had become so strained that it would be very difficult for the two nations to compete against one another in future without unpleasant incidents.

Sullivan, in his capacity as the president of the American Olympic Committee and head of the AAU, was the driving force behind the criticism. He had no hesitation in accusing British officials of being unfair to every athlete except their own, but emphasised that their real aim was to beat the Americans.

"Their conduct," he said, "was cruel and unsportsmanlike and absolutely unfair" (Killanin & Rodda – *The Olympic Games*). He informed the *New York Times* that, "so far as I am personally concerned this is the last international meeting I shall recommend the Americans to take part in until assured that every country competing shall have some say in the management, so that we shall not hereafter be placed in the false position that we have here".

In September 1908 a fresh broadside was fired against the British by Gustavus Kirby, another member of the American Olympic Committee and a staunch ally of Sullivan. He gave a speech in New York in which he publicly criticised the Games' officials and the British media attacks on the conduct of the American team. He ensured his speech was followed up by preparing a provocative pamphlet setting out in detail his accusations. In all, they fell under the following main headings:

The absence of the American flag at the opening day of the Games;

The poor arrangement of the event programme;

The method of drawing the heats;

The rules relating to the pole vault and high jump;

The coaching by the British officials;

The decision in the 400 metre race;

The protests over the marathon race, and the Longboat entry;

The conduct of the British officials towards the American committee.

Kirby maintained that the British Olympic Association's response to these criticisms had been nothing more than implied admittances, excuses or half-hearted apologies, or even, for example in the case of the 400 metre race, simply untrue (Mallon and Buchanan – *The 1908 Olympic Games*).

British officials were stunned by the venom of

the American attacks. Even de Coubertin expressed his concern. "I just could not understand Sullivan's attitude here", he wrote. "He shared his team's frenzy and did nothing to try to calm them down" (Guttman – *The Olympics*).

The recriminations took another twist when an American lawyer, Francis Peabody, who was present at the Games but had no official status, used a Boston newspaper to defend the British and to refute Kirby's comments. Predictably, he simply provoked a fiercer American response. A thirty-five page pamphlet attacking Peabody as well as the British Olympic Committee was drawn up by "A Member of the American Olympic Committee", probably either Kirby himself or Sullivan.

The British sporting authorities could no longer delay making a formal response. It came late in 1908 when the British Olympic Association published a sixty-page report entitled *The Olympic Games of 1908 in London: A Reply to Certain Criticisms*. It was put together by the assiduous Theodore Cook, who was also the editor of the official report on the London Olympiad.

The report did not mince its words. It freely acknowledged that the American team were indeed the finest body of athletes who had ever visited this country. However, they would, it declared, go down in history as the team who made more complaints than ever before in the Games, and who had gone home moreover without a word of thanks for the hospitality the British authorities had shown them.

Although the Association had not wanted to be drawn into the controversy, the statements made in America, especially in the press, were, it said, "of such a character they cannot pass unchallenged".

The Association had no doubt that the blame for much of the trouble rested personally with James Sullivan, Gustavus Kirby and their friends. It pointed out that if just one quarter of the accusations they levelled at British officials had been true, then it could not be imagined that "any of our visitors would have given our meeting the support of their presence for a single day".

It was stressed that none of the other nations competing under British officials at the stadium programme had indirectly or directly ever endorsed a single word of the blame, "so freely showered upon us by some of the American officials". In fact this was not true. Both France and Sweden, for example, had lodged fairly serious complaints during the course of the Games.

A large part of the report incorporated the official response of the Amateur Athletic Association. It, too, had been deeply angered by what it dismissed as the "unfair and untrue" statements appearing in the American press, and in speeches made by the American Olympic officials who had been present at the Games.

Some of the criticisms, such as officials deliber-ately fixing the heats so that more British athletes could qualify, and the accusation that officials had hit the marathon runner, Hayes, as he came to the tape, were simply dismissed by the Association as lies or falsehoods. But the Association gave close and detailed attention to the controversies relating to the absence of the American flag at the opening ceremony, to the 400 metres and to the marathon.

The AAA drew heavily on signed statements from officials and competitors to answer the complaints made by the Americans. Unfortunately, the overall impression was one-sided, and the rather heavy and lordly tone of the report did nothing to placate the Americans and merely heightened the tension between the two countries.

As neither side was prepared to back down, further recriminations followed. The rift between the British and American sporting bodies became steadily more serious. Finally, at their 1909 convention, the American Amateur Athletic Union voted to break off relations with the Amateur Athletic Association.

In practice, the breach did not entirely restrict competition between individuals of the two countries, but it was not until 1922 that a letter of agreement was signed formally restoring amicable relations between the two organisations (Mallon & Buchanan – *The 1908 Olympic Games*).

Interestingly, a year after Theodore Cook had drawn up the British report he was elected a member of the IOC. He resigned in 1915 when he failed to get sufficient support for his proposal that Germany should be excluded from the Olympic movement. He was said to have spent much time in later life in maintaining good relations between sportsmen in England and America.

In the final analysis, both Great Britain and America could draw considerable satisfaction from their success at the London Games. The American athletes had achieved their objective of dominating the prestigious track and field events, where the United States took fifteen out of the twenty-seven gold medals. But Britain, with its total of fifty-six gold medals in all competitions, was by far the most successful country overall. It is the first and only time that Britain has won more medals than any other nation.

Chapter 9

The Olympians

"As the athletes dispersed many of us who watched them felt that we were never likely to look upon so splendid a set of men again."
– Theodore Cook, Official Olympic report.

On the afternoon of Saturday July 25th 1908, after twelve days of intense sporting activity, the stadium Games came to a close when the Closing and Awards ceremony was held. No fewer than one thousand three hundred and twenty trophies and cups, medals and diplomas, were awarded to a great host of athletes and officials. Even the participants in the demonstration events were not forgotten, and they received their commemorative medals. Since by now King Edward had refused to have anything more to do with the Games, it fell to Queen Alexandra to make the presentation of the gold medals. As the band of the Grenadier Guards struck up "See, the Conquering Hero Comes", the new Olympic champions advanced across the grass to the Queen to receive their gold medals and a sprig of oak leaves from Windsor forest tied in red, white and blue ribbons. The South African 100 metre sprint champion led the procession and as the rest followed one after another the official Olympic Report declared that "the spectators realised that they were looking at the finest procession of athletes which had ever passed before a Queen".

It was a relaxed, festive and happy occasion, with the tensions of the previous days over. Even the rains had stopped and the weather was bright and warm. To cheers and laughter, Lord Desborough was presented with his commemorative medal by his wife. Johnny Hayes had received the marathon trophy to warm applause, and he was carried shoulder high on a table around the stadium by his jubilant team-mates. And then it was the turn of Dorando Pietri to receive his special cup from the hands of the Queen to "salvoes of cheers which must have been heard miles away" (*The Sporting Life*).

The final official banquets were held, the tributes paid and the flowery speeches made. The athletes, dignitaries and officials departed, and the great stadium soon turned to other uses. Memories too would fade, and feuds were eventually forgotten. But for a short space of time, the hopes and aspirations, and triumphs and failures, of many people became inextricably linked with the drama and glory of the London Olympiad. It is to some of those people that we now turn.

On the first Sunday of the 1908 Games, Ethelbert Talbot, the Bishop of Pennsylvania, had given a sermon at St Paul's cathedral in which he uttered the words that became symbolic of the Games – "What is important in these Olympic Games is not to win as to take part". The words are often inaccurately attributed to de Coubertin. However, he was so impressed with them that he expanded upon them later to make his famous remark that "What is important in life is not victory but the battle. What matters is not to have won, but to have fought well."

The portraits that follow are of nine men and one woman who "fought well" at the London Olympics, and indeed throughout their lives. Not all won gold medals, and one, Lord Desborough, although a remarkable sportsman and himself a former Olympian, did not actually compete in London. Several of them were to die tragically young. But all were heroes, and all achieved fame at some time, however fleeting, and the story of their lives and achievements deserves to be told.

Chapter 10

Man of Affairs and Lover of Games
Lord Desborough

"Always one thinks of Lord Desborough in connection with mountain peaks, sounding seas, wild deserts, winding country roads, smooth-shaven cricket greens, and the tree-shaded reaches of the river. He is a sportsman of the open air, the ideal Englishman – a man of affairs, a lover of games. The nation is fortunate in such a citizen." – Fry's Magazine, July 1906.

William Henry Grenfell, later Lord Desborough, was a distinguished British amateur sportsman, public figure and adventurer. He was born in London in 1855. He was the eldest son of Charles William Grenfell MP and Georgiana Caroline Lascelles. A very influential and popular figure in his time, he is now perhaps better known as the father of the war poet Julian Grenfell.

A man of great natural authority and practical good sense, he was widely respected for his sporting achievements and for his many contributions to public life. He was a man who could always "get things done", and without his drive and organisational skills the London Games would never have opened on time.

Physically, he was a tall man, more than six foot, with broad shoulders and a deep chest. His photographs show he had a rather hard and forbidding look about him but, it was said, there was always "a pleasant gleam in his eyes, and a smile is never far from his lips" (*Fry's Magazine*). He had a quick sense of humour and was a modest, friendly and generous man. After the London marathon, he sent flowers to Pietri wishing him a speedy recovery from his ordeal, and he personally paid for the gold medals of the American shooting team to be replaced after they had been stolen.

Willy Grenfell, as he was known, attended Harrow School and Balliol College, Oxford, graduating in 1879. He quickly showed outstanding sporting ability.

He represented Harrow at cricket, being awarded the school bowling and catching prizes, and won the school mile in 4 min 37 secs, a time which stood as a school record for more than sixty years. At Oxford he represented the university in rowing, fencing and athletics. Whilst at Oxford he successfully climbed the Matterhorn by three different routes.

He was a prodigious rower. He rowed for Oxford against Cambridge in the classic boat race in 1877 which resulted in a dead heat, and in the 1878 crew

Huge crowds watch the cycling at the White City.

Lord Desborough makes a speech at the Henley rowing events.

The Henley events get under way.

South African Reggie Walker is carried on the shoulders of his supporters after his 100 metres victory.

John Carpenter of the USA whose tactics led to his disqualification in the 400 metres final.

Wyndham Halswelle wins the 400 metres in solitary splendour.

Mel Sheppard (USA) beats Harold Wilson (GB) in the 1500 metres.

Johnny Hayes wins the marathon.

Dorando Pietri gets some consolation for his disqualification from the marathon by receiving a gold cup from Queen Alexandra.

Martin Sheridan, the outspoken captain of the US team.

Ralph Rose, the man who upset the King.

Alfred Gilbert (USA) clears the bar at 3.71m to tie for the gold medal in the pole vault.

USA's Ray Ewry on his way to high jump gold, his tenth Olympic gold in all.

Henry Taylor is carried aloft.as his delighted team mates run alongside.

The triumphant British football team.

*Sweden's Ulrich Salchow, gold medallist and inventor
of the Salchow jump.*

which won by ten lengths. He was elected President of the Oxford University Boat Club. After leaving the university he won the Grand Challenge Cup at Henley in 1881. Later, he won the Thames punting championships for three successive years (1888–90). He stroked an eight in a boat from Dover to Calais in 1885, taking great care to ensure that each crew member had a jam pot to bail out water. In 1889 he sculled with two others from Oxford to Putney in twenty-two hours, a distance of more than one hundred miles, overcoming blisters and violent muscular contractions.

A strong swimmer, Desborough tested himself by swimming across the pool at the foot of the Niagara Falls in 1884, and then again in 1888, this time in a snowstorm. It was said that he repeated the feat to prove to a distinguished, but sceptical, American lawyer that he had in fact done it the first time. At one point in the swim he found himself being pulled by the backwash dangerously close to the falls which he saw above his head. But he struck out for the middle and finally reached the Canadian side. Even he admitted later that "I really did think something might go wrong" (*Fry's Magazine*).

Asked later by a friend if his wife was proud of him, he replied, "No, not at all! She pretended to be terribly angry with me, and demanded to know why I had tried to make her a widow!" (*Fry's Magazine*). For many years he was president of the Royal Life Saving Society, and as president of the Thames Conservancy Board – a post he held for thirty-two years – he arranged for all the river lock-keepers to be trained to save and resuscitate people in difficulty.

He was a very keen horseman, hunter and fisherman. As master of the draghounds at Oxford he kept his own harriers at his home, Taplow Court. Whilst hunting in the Rockies in 1888 he became lost for two days. Unperturbed, in the evenings he read the entire works of Milton by the light of a candle on a stick. He hunted tigers and elephants in India and at one time had to flee for his life when chased by a mad elephant. In the space of three weeks he caught one hundred tarpon in Florida in 1899, the largest weighing one hundred and eighty-two pound. During 1916, he made a strong contribution to the Venison Committee which had been established to overcome wartime food shortages, when he stalked and shot eighty stags.

As a fencer, he won the Foils at Harrow and Oxford. He represented England in four international competitions, including the Athens Games of 1906, where, though fifty years old and weighing fourteen stones, in the words of his team captain, "he fought like a Trojan". He was the founding president of the Amateur Fencing Association.

At various other times, Lord Desborough was president of the Amateur Athletic Association, as well as president of the Lawn Tennis Association and the Marylebone Cricket Club, and a founding member of the Queen's Tennis Club.

Given his family background, Willy Grenfell was always likely to play a prominent part in public life. On leaving Oxford he was immediately invited to stand as Liberal candidate at Salisbury and was elected to parliament in 1880. During his political career he served as private secretary to the chancellor of the exchequer, Sir William Harcourt, but later left the Liberal Party to become a Conservative in protest over the Home Rule for Ireland bill. In 1905 he was elevated to the peerage as Baron Desborough of Taplow.

Although Desborough did not reach high political office, and declined for family reasons the offer in 1921 of the Governor-Generalship of Canada, he was an extremely hard-working public servant. He was said at one time to be serving on no fewer than one hundred and fifteen committees! He filled almost all the important offices open to him in local government and local justice in the counties of Berkshire and Buckinghamshire. The number of important public appointments he held and their variety is very impressive. He had also been president of the London Chamber of Commerce, the British Imperial Chamber of Commerce, as well as chairing the Home Office Committee on Police of England, Scotland and Wales.

During the First World War he was very active as the president of the Central Association of Volunteer Training Corps in which at time one or another more than a million men served, most of whom were either too old for military service or in protected occupations. The Corps played an important part in releasing trained troops for active service, as well as helping to bring in the harvest and working in dockyards and munitions factories.

In 1906 Lord Desborough returned from the Athenian Games, in which he had been a member of the British fencing team, with the invitation that Britain should take over the organisation of the 1908 Games. He consulted King Edward VII and the big sporting associations, and on November 19th 1906, a letter was despatched to the International Olympic Committee formally accepting that London should became the host city for the IV Olympiad.

When the members of the newly formed British Olympic Council received the news that Britain was to host the 1908 Games, they were confident that in Desborough they had the man to lead the formidable task ahead. His drive and organisational talents, and of course his sporting achievements, made him the ideal man to prepare the country for the Olympiad. He possessed, said one council member, "the skill of a D'Artagnan, the strength of a Porthos, the heart of an Athos, and the body of an Englishman" (*The News*).

Just as important too was the fact that Desborough had the personality that the Council recognised would be important to the success of the Games. He was courteous, well-connected and popular. He was unpretentious. As the magazine *The Empire* said, he was "Utterly devoid of arrogance, or side, which frequently causes Englishmen to be detested by the foreigner". To navigate around the elaborate social structure of the age, someone was needed who could be trusted to win the support and confidence, not only of the host of visiting royalty and dignitaries, but all classes of people in the country.

A man, as one council member put it, who would guarantee that, "every humble subject of this country who had a shilling left in his pocket on Saturday, or any day of the week, might be able to spend that shilling with the certain knowledge that he would get his money's worth of true sport" (Official Report). They found such a man in Willy Desborough.

Appointed as the president of the Olympic organising committee, Desborough, now fifty-one, had less than two years to organise the London Games. From the start, he was personally involved in all aspects of the Games. For him, they were in effect "the actualisation of a dream".

Great Britain was acknowledged to be the cradle of athletic sports, and Desborough believed that it was absolutely essential that the Olympics were carried out in a manner worthy of a great athletic nation. In the work ahead, he was fortunate to have the services alongside him of the indefatigable council secretary, the Rev Courcy Laffan, who shared his energy and enthusiasm for the Olympics.

Desborough was described by *Throne* magazine in 1908 as "the real hero of the Olympiad". He lifted the first girder of the new White City stadium into place himself. He made innumerable speeches, hosted banquets and entertained at Taplow Court. He dealt untiringly and with good humour with countless meetings, some of which on occasions, it was said, lasted a week without a break! He was the man who persuaded Lord Northcliffe to launch the public campaign that saved the finances of the Games. His wife, Lady Desborough, acted as hostess at official functions on many occasions, and together with the Queen was one of those who distributed medals at the closing ceremony.

He was also deeply committed to the wider mission of the Olympic movement. In a later review of the Games, he reflected eloquently about the expression of good fellowship between Greek and Greek which had characterised the original Olympic Games, and which enabled the Hellenic race to put aside their internal bickering and conflicts and co-operate peacefully. He believed the same ideals could be applied to the modern world from international athletics.

The two thousand young men and women from various countries who had taken part in the London Games were, he wrote, "inspired by the same ideals of physical excellence and committed with each other in friendly rivalry. These young men are also representatives of the generation into whose hands the destinies of most of the world are passing at the moment, and with them the hopes of international peace (Official Report).

Fine words, but as we have seen the Americans at the time did not, unfortunately, see it quite like that. Privately, Lord Desborough was upset by the controversies that surrounded the Games, but he refused to indulge in public recriminations, and he responded to criticisms carefully and with dignity. He emerged from the Games with his reputation nationally and internationally unharmed, and, with Laffan, is truly one of the two great pillars on which the British Olympic movement has been built.

In 1887, Lord Desborough had married Ethel Anne Fane. Together they made Taplow Court on the banks of the Thames a highly fashionable society venue. Ettie Grenfell was a brilliant hostess and a leading member of the politically minded group of intellectuals known as The Souls. They had five much-loved children, three boys and two girls. The two eldest sons were killed in action in 1915 and the third son died in 1926 as the result of a motor car accident. The death of his sons affected Lord Desborough deeply and he gradually withdrew from public life. But he never lost his interest in sporting matters and loved to talk about them. In the 1930's the writer Lytton Strachey described him as still "a huge rock of an athlete".

Lord Desborough died in 1945 in his ninetieth year. Early reports of his death had been grossly exaggerated. There are reports he was infuriated one day in 1920 to find his obituary that had been printed in *The Times*, rather than that of his near namesake Lord Bessborough who had just died. He promptly called the editor. "Look here," he cried, "You've published my obituary this morning!" "I'm sorry," the editor is alleged to have replied, "but from where are you speaking, my Lord?"

Chapter 11

Soldier Athlete
Wyndham Halswelle

"The sport he graced with such style will ensure he is remembered for ever." – Doug Gillon, journalist, Glasgow Herald.

Wyndham Halswelle, the winner of the controversial 400 metres at the London Olympics, was a brilliant middle distance runner whose life came to a tragic end in the Great War. He remains the only British athlete to have the full collection of gold, silver and bronze medals in individual events.

Halswelle, like another famous Scottish athlete, Eric Liddell, was not in fact born in Scotland but in London in 1882. He came from a well-to-do family. He was the youngest son of the successful and distinguished painter, Keeley Halswelle, and a Scottish mother, Helen Gordon, from whom he derived his Scottish qualification. His maternal grandfather was General Nathaniel Gordon (no relation to General Gordon of Khartoum fame) who served in the Indian Army. Wyndham was sent to Sunningdale School in Berkshire and then to Charterhouse School where he soon showed great promise as a runner from anything from 100 yards to one mile. Destined for a military career, in 1900 he went to the Royal Military College, Sandhurst, where he continued to impress in athletics.

In 1901 he was commissioned in the Highland Light Infantry and was soon posted off to fight in the Boer War in South Africa. In the Transvaal he served not as a footsoldier but on horseback in the regiment's Mounted Infantry Company. He was very active in the various operations of the company and in 1902 received the Queen's Medal with four clasps. Whenever he had the opportunity he participated in the regimental sports.

It was in South Africa that his exceptional powers as an athlete were noticed by Jimmy Curran, a former professional athlete from Galashiels and later a successful coach in America. Curran persuaded Halswelle to apply himself seriously to running and took him under his wing. With proper training and coaching Halswelle soon made up for lost time. Regarded more as a "strider" than an out and out sprinter, it was when he approached the 300 metre mark that his strength and speed showed he had world championship class.

Returning with his regiment to Britain in 1904, Halswelle in the same year won the Army 880 yards title. In 1905 he won both the Scottish AAA and AAA 440 yards titles. At the Athens Olympics in 1906 he had his first taste of international success. Such was the progress he had made that he went to those interim Games as the pre-race favourite for the 400 metres. But he was just beaten into second place by the fast-finishing American, Paul Pilgrim. Halswelle was anxious to make up for his disappointment in the 800 metre final, but once again Pilgrim won the race and Halswelle had to settle for third place.

On his return to Scotland he produced a phenomenal piece of running by winning the 100, 220, 440 and 880 yard races against formidable opposition in one afternoon at the Scottish Championships at Powderhall. Two weeks later he retained his AAA 440 title in a best time of 48.8 seconds which was not beaten until 1934. A leg injury meant that Halswelle competed little in 1907, but he returned fresh to the track in 1908. His hard training for the Olympic year paid off, and he soon established a new world record for the 300 yards which survived until 1961 when it was beaten by a Glasgow University student, Menzies Campbell, later the leader of the Liberal Democrat party.

At the peak of his condition, Hallswelle looked forward eagerly to the London Olympics in July. Although strongly fancied for the 800 metres as well, it was the 400 metres for which he was selected.

He was conscious he had the hopes of the nation on his shoulders. This was a distance at which, then as now, the Americans had a high reputation and were to be strongly represented. No other event at the Games represented more the intense rivalry between the British and American teams.

In the final on July 23rd at 5.30pm, Halswelle lined up against three fine American athletes before a large and excited crowd. As described in the earlier chapter on the race itself, the stage was set for one of the most dramatic clashes in the history of the Games and one that was to do much to tear apart the sporting relationship of the two countries.

The controversy that surrounded the event was a huge personal disappointment for Wyndham Halswelle. He was enormously popular with spectators, who appreciated his prowess as a runner and his fair-minded and gracious manner. He had no wish to let them down but he wanted to win fairly in competition. He was very reluctant to run the "walkover" arranged following Carpenter's disqualification and the withdrawal of the other two Americans, but the AAA gave him no option and insisted that he should run around the track on his own. It was cruel that a runner of his stature was obliged to win his gold medal in such unfortunate and demeaning circumstances.

Although at the peak of his powers, the Olympic experience left Halswelle disillusioned with the sport, and he gave up running shortly after. An American promoter tried to tempt him into a grudge re-match with John Carpenter in New Jersey but he would have none of it. He made his farewell appearance in the 1908 Glasgow Rangers Sports event at Ibrox Park. He never ran publicly again and concentrated on his army career. He was promoted to captain in September 1911. His meticulously kept diaries show him to be an extremely conscientious officer with a deep interest in the welfare, training and safety of his men.

Seven years later, in March 1915, Wyndham Halswelle lost his life in the Great War at the battle of Neuve Chapelle whilst serving as a captain with the Highland Light Infantry. In the regiment's chronicle, he has left a graphic account of the fighting at the battle leading up to his own death. He described the horrors of trench warfare: "I called on the men to get over the parapet. There is great difficulty in getting out of a trench, especially for small men laden with a pack, rifle and perhaps 50 rounds in the pouch, and a bandolier of 50 rounds hung around them, and perhaps four feet of slippery clay perpendicular with sandbags on top. I got three men hit actually on top of the parapet".

He made a dash at the parapet but fell back. "The Jocks then heaved me up and I jumped into a ditch, filled with liquid mud, which took me some time to get out of" (*Glasgow Herald* magazine, August 12th 2006).

In this assault, seventy-five men died to gain fifteen yards before his company retreated to the position from which they had started. They spent the night with no water or stretchers and had to carry the wounded by hand. The following day Halswelle was himself wounded when a bullet went through a man's head and struck him on the temple. He was hospitalised but soon bravely insisted on returning to the front line. Within days he was dead. He walked along a trench, giving encouragement and instructions to his men, but there were parts where it was dangerous to walk upright safely. A sniper took an opportunity to shoot him above the temple. He died shortly afterwards and was buried locally on a farm. Later his body was exhumed and re-interred in the Royal Irish Rifles graveyard in the village of Laventie, not far from Armentieres.

Halswelle was only thirty-two when he died. He never married. Every year since 1969 in memory of his name his regiment, now the Royal Highland Fusiliers, awards the Wyndham Halswelle Memorial Trophy to the winner of the 400 metres at the Scottish Junior Championships. In 2003 he was one of fifty inaugural inductees into the Scottish Sports Hall of Fame. Scotland has also established an Athletics Hall of Fame, and in 2006 Halswelle became its fourth inductee behind Allan Wells, Eric Liddell and Liz McColgan. Fittingly, on the induction occasion, the Guest of Honour was the American athlete, Michael Johnson, who dominated 400 metres running for many years.

Chapter 12

The Bohola Boy
Martin Sheridan

"Sheridan was without question the greatest athlete this country has ever known." New York Times.

The Irish American Martin Sheridan was a legendary figure in the athletics world in the early 1900s. He competed at the 1904, 1906 and 1908 Olympics and won a total of five gold medals. During the course of his illustrious career he established sixteen world records. At the London Games he was given the honour of captaining the American Olympic team. A very modest personality, he retained a deep love for his Irish heritage.

He was born at a farm in Bohola, County Mayo, in 1881. Bohola remains today a small village, but close-knit community, of around twenty houses. Jim Clarke, a cousin of Sheridan, who also won a silver medal in the 1908 Games, was born in the village as well, so Bohola, it is said, has the proud boast of having produced winners of more Olympic medals per head of the population than anywhere else in the world.

The farm was relatively large and so was the family – three brothers and two sisters. There were plenty of jobs on the farm to keep them all occupied. The village children had to create their own entertainment, and on summer evenings they gathered together to play games such as pitch and toss, throwing weights and other pastimes. The local policemen also took part in the games and gave the children helpful advice on such things as throwing techniques. It was here that Sheridan learned some of the basic skills in weight-throwing so invaluable to him in his later years as a champion discus thrower.

Prospects of work were poor in Ireland, so in 1899, at the age of eighteen, Martin Sheridan emigrated to America, following in the footsteps of his older brother, Richard, who had emigrated a few years earlier. Once they were settled, the two brothers took the civil service examinations and, like many Irishmen before them, joined the police force in New York. Since both men were keen sportsmen, they quickly took full advantage of the training facilities available to policemen and they competed together at the local athletic clubs.

Richard Sheridan had already established a reputation as one of America's leading discus throwers and Martin was inspired to take up the event. It soon became obvious that his strength, speed, and accuracy as a thrower were exceptional and he had the potential to be the best in the world at it. Martin was now six foot three inches in height and in his prime, a fairly lean one hundred and ninety-five pounds. He developed the novel technique of making two turns in the discus circle which gave him an advantage over his competitors who made only a turn and a half. When he and Richard were joined by another brother, Andrew, the Sheridans regularly created a sensation in athletic events by taking the first three places!

At that time many of the top weight throwers in the world were Irish immigrants, and Sheridan took his place among the group of athletes known as the "Irish Whales" because of their impressive size and weight. Although he was at his peak as a discus thrower when there was no official governing body recognising world records, it was generally accepted that he set his first world mark on September 14th 1901 when he threw the discus 120ft 10¾in (36.77m) at a small competition in Patterson, New Jersey. Other successes were soon to follow and he remained unbeatable for several years. He seemed to be able to produce a world record throw almost every time he picked up the discus. In all, he is credited with no fewer than fifteen new "world bests" in the discus. His last world record was made at the Celtic Park, New York, in October 1909 when he threw 142ft 10¼ins (41.46 metres).

Sheridan had a phenomenal Olympic record. He made his debut when he was just twenty-three at the 1904 St Louis Olympics. He was expected to do well in the discus but the competition was tough, and he found himself in third place before the final three rounds. He summoned up all his strength, and on his fifth throw managed to tie for the lead with Richard Rose, another American and the world's leading shot-putter. For the only time in Olympic history a throw-off was ordered to decide the medals, and it was Sheridan who went on to take the gold medal with a throw of 127ft 10¼in (39.00m)

The 1906 interim games in Athens were the scene of his greatest all-round athletic performance. He was a member of the first official United States team, and their journey to Athens was long and arduous. Their ship hit rough weather in the Atlantic and on one occasion a huge wave swept over the bow and smashed a group of the American team against the deck and rails. Sheridan was among the athletes who were injured seriously enough to require medical attention (Schaap – *An Illustrated History of the Olympics*).

He made a swift recovery and entered fourteen events at the Athens Games, although competing in only seven of them. His performance was the highlight of the Games. He beat the Greek national champion to win the discus gold medal by throwing a world record of 136ft (41.46m). He also won the gold in the shot put, although rather luckily as the Finnish competitor, Jaervinnen, was disqualified because it was judged he had "thrown" the shot.

Sheridan went on to win three silver medals – in the stone throw, the standing high jump and the standing long jump. However, a knee injury prevented him from completing the pentathlon in which he would have almost certainly taken a third gold medal at Athens. As well as his prowess in the field events, he was no mean performer on the track and could run the 100 yards in a little over ten seconds. He later described his withdrawal from the Athens pentathlon as the greatest disappointment in his athletic career.

King George of Greece was so impressed with Martin Sheridan's all-round performance that he had a statue erected in the Irishman's honour in Athens, and presented him with a gold goblet and vaulting pole.

Sheridan returned to New York where he was acclaimed as the greatest track and field athlete of all time. He continued to post new world records, and as a result of his prodigious display in the American trials in June 1908 for the London Games, he was made captain of the American team and selected for every field event, including the tug of war.

On his arrival in London he was asked what he thought of the American chances in the Games, and joked that his team would take seventy-five per cent of the prizes and "knock the socks off the British". He certainly played his part. He won three medals, a gold for each of the discus and the Greek-style discus throws, and a bronze medal for the standing long jump. In other events he was less successful. An injury forced him to withdraw from the triple jump, and in the shot put he finished eleventh. The American tug of war team consisted of their top weight throwers, including Sheridan, but they had no chance against the much more experienced Liverpool police team, especially in their hobnailed boots!

Sheridan was a modest, open and easy-going character who disliked any discussion about his own achievements. But he loved his mother country passionately, and felt strongly about what he considered the injustices done to Ireland and whenever possible defended her interests.

In London he was one of those who demanded that Irish athletes should be allowed to have their own national recognition at the Olympics. He was particularly scathing about British values of sport and fair play and later told an Irish audience that "the treatment meted out to our athletes in the London stadium will not soon be forgotten".

He was, of course, party to the controversy that broke out when Ralph Rose failed to dip the American Flag when the American team passed the Royal Box. Sheridan has often been accused of being himself the flag bearer but that was not the case. The mistake seems to have arisen from Sheridan's famous remark a few days later when questioned about the incident, that the flag dipped to no earthly king.

After the London Games Sheridan hoped to go back quietly to Ireland and to surprise his family at Bohola. But news of his arrival in Ireland travelled fast and he was greeted very enthusiastically wherever he went. When he reached Bohola on August 2nd 1908 he was given a rapturous open air reception. The chairman of the welcoming committee, Rev John O'Grady, warmly greeted the "All Round Champion of the World – this young Bohola boy who comes back to us after a comparative few years' absence" (*The Martin Sheridan Story*).

A formal address to Sheridan, signed by the priests and people of his native parish of Bohola, was then read out by John Doyle, a teacher. No praise was too high.

It was noted that "Greece had her Leander, Rome her Spartacus, and Scotland her Wallace, all men of great strength and physical prowess but it remained for Ireland to turn out the greatest athlete of them all. … With all your athletic triumphs, we feel that you have not yet arrived at the climax of what your majestic manhood is capable of, and we hope in the future to hear of victories still greater than those you have already won."

Sheridan, who was an eloquent man, responded by thanking everyone for the "beautiful address". It was, he said, "no great distinction for an Irishman to be a champion. The Irishmen are remarkable in every part of the world for their athletic powers".

Before he left Ireland, Sheridan competed in a number of athletic events before large crowds. His appearance at the Ballina Sports in Co Mayo drew one of the largest sporting crowds ever seen in Ireland.

There was such a rush of people to see the "genial Bohola giant" that the ticket collectors had to abandon efforts at collecting entrance money. Sheridan did not disappoint his spectators, winning several events before establishing a new world record for throwing the 7lb weight.

He was given a huge send-off when he left Swinford Station in Co Mayo on September 8th to join his liner bound for the United States. As his train moved off he turned to some of the young men there and said, "Goodbye, boys. I thank you from the bottom of my heart and I hope to be back again amongst you before this time twelve months". He was, however, never to return.

On returning to the US, he continued to compete in athletics until forced to retire after contracting blood poisoning which very nearly took his life. However, he remained active in the sporting world as an adviser and coach, and also as a promoter of athletic games to help the families of policemen who had died in service.

As a police officer he was highly thought of and reached the rank of first grade detective sergeant in the New York Police Department. He was a man of the highest integrity and a very brave policeman. Once in his early years on patrol, he came upon a house on fire and saved four children and their parents from certain death. Whenever Governor Glynn of New York visited the city, it would be Sheridan who was selected to be his personal bodyguard.

He never married and died tragically young. In 1918 he contracted pneumonia working a double shift for a sick colleague and passed away on the day before his thirty-seventh birthday. Great crowds thronged the streets through which his funeral procession passed. It was reported that, "the funeral was of modest character in keeping with the personality of the former Olympic champion" (*New York Times*).

Two weeks after his funeral more than five hundred people gathered at the Irish American Athletic Club to discuss how some suitable memorial to his achievements could be made. Several thousands of dollars were pledged, and finally in 1921 a monument to his memory was unveiled at the Calvary cemetery in New York in the shape of a Celtic Cross.

In 1988, America made a fitting tribute to a very great athlete when Martin Sheridan was inducted into the National Track and Field Hall of Fame located at Indianapolis. Nor have the achievements of Sheridan been forgotten in Ireland by his local community. In 1966 a memorial was unveiled in Bohola, and in 1994 the community raised enough funds to open the Sheridan Memorial Community Centre.

Chapter 13

The Man who upset the King
Ralph Rose

"Boyish patriotism! The Spirit of 1776!
Nonsense. Sheer, caddish, boorish manners."
– The Bookman, October 1908.

Ralph Waldo Rose was one of the greatest athletes ever produced on the west coast of America and an outstanding Olympic champion. His speciality was the shot put. Over a span of eight years he won many major championships. He became the first man to break the fifty-foot barrier for the shot put and in 1909 set a world record of 54ft 4ins (16.56m) that was not beaten until 1934.

He was born in Healdsburg, California, in March 1885. He was the son of an attorney, and attended the local high school. He went on to attend the University of Michigan but did not graduate. At the university he was apparently not "relished" by the better class of students and his scholastic career there was ended after some rowdy behaviour. He later attended Chicago University where he studied law and was admitted to the bar. He practised later in his home town.

Whilst at Michigan he became interested in athletics and became a member of the university track team. He was a very big man – six foot six inches tall and weighing two hundred and ninety-five pounds – and not surprisingly attracted the attention of the coach of the university football team. Reportedly, however, he did not prove fast enough for coach Fielding "Hurry Up" Yost's so-called point a minute team.

Rose concentrated on the throwing events and quickly demonstrated his considerable ability in a sporting activity that was particularly popular before the First World War. Whilst still at Michigan he became the Pacific Coast champion in the 16-pound shot put, the 16-pound hammer throw, and the discus. He later joined the San Francisco Olympic Club and went on to win seven AAU titles in the shot, discus and javelin, and continued to set new world record marks.

He was to compete in three Olympic Games, winning three golds, two silvers and a bronze. In his first Games in St Louis he won the shot with a world record (48ft 7ins, 14.80m), and took second place in the discus and third in the hammer throw. By the time of the London Games four years later he had become a veritable giant of a man of more than three hundred pounds, and in pouring rain and treacherous conditions he comfortably won the shot with a throw of 46ft 7ins (14.18m). The silver medallist in the event was Denis Horgan, a thirty-seven-year-old Irishman who competed for Great Britain. Although well past his prime, Horgan's achievement was all the more remarkable since he had been almost killed just the year before. On duty as a policeman in New York, he had tried to break up a brawl and been severely beaten with sticks and shovels.

For all Rose's athletic triumphs, it was at the London Games that he achieved his most lasting claim to fame by setting the tradition that the American flag is never to be dipped at the opening ceremonies of the Olympics. Initially, it was the American team captain, Martin Sheridan, who had been selected to carry the US flag at the opening parade of the American athletes but he was replaced at the last minute by Rose. The reason for this is not clear. Maybe it was to conserve Sheridan's energy for competition later, or possibly the Americans were not sure that the republican Sheridan, representing the Irish American Athletic Club, could be counted upon to show proper respect towards King Edward. As it happened, when Rose passed the Royal Stand, he was the one who failed to dip the American flag as protocol required. When challenged later about the incident, Rose expressed his innocence, claiming that: "I was never told what to do" (Mallon and Buchanan – *The 1908 Olympic Games*).

This may have been the case, but there had been rehearsals for the march past, and it is odd, too, that he chose to do nothing when all the other delegations around him were either lowering their flags or making their salutes.

At the time the incident received little attention in the British and American press, and only later came to be blown up as a calculated affront to the King and the British people. However, the failure to dip the flag had not gone unnoticed by the British crowd and very probably precipitated some of the resentment shown by some spectators towards the American competitors during the Games.

The incident did, of course, also give rise to the legendary remark attributed to Martin Sheridan that "This flag dips to no earthly king". In fact, it was only some fifty years later that the media started to make use of the remark, and the eminent sports historians – Mallon and Buchanan – found no evidence to support the view that it was Sheridan who actually said it in public. Nonetheless, in one way or another, it was Rose's inaction which has established the tradition that the American flag is not to be lowered at Olympic opening ceremonies.

Rose made his final appearance at the 1912 Stockholm Olympics. He led a team of huge American weight throwers the like of which had never been seen before in Europe. It was at these Games that Rose was said to eat two pounds of steak for his breakfast and six eggs in their shells! He duly won the right hand – left hand shot put with a total of 90ft 52ins (28.75m). But he had to concede first place in the shot put to the mighty American policeman, Pat McDonald, who weighed in at around three hundred and fifty pounds.

Ralph Rose never married. He was reported to be

"a big, florid and full-blooded man", who enjoyed life, but he died after a brief illness from typhoid fever in 1913 at the early age of twenty-nine. James Sullivan, the American Olympic Commissioner, paid tribute to Rose, whose death was a severe blow to athletes, to Americans, and as one whose presence in future Games would be badly missed. Rose was inducted into the United States National Track and Field Hall of Fame in 1976.

Chapter 14

Dorando and Johnny
Marathon runners

"The reason why Dorando does not win is that the day before the marathon he eats Irish beef stew instead of spaghetti. Ironically, Hayes was the son of Irish immigrants."
– Irving Berlin, composer, drawn from his lyric entitled Dorando.

The legendary Dorando Pietri was born in Mandrio, a district of Corregio, in the north of Italy in May 1885. His father was a peasant farmer who had to work hard in the fields to support his wife and his four sons. In 1897, he decided the economic prospects looked better in the neighbouring town of Carpi and settled there with his family, opening a fruit and vegetable store.

At the age of fourteen, Pietri became an apprentice pastry cook. He was an active boy, and in his spare time first took up cycling before turning to the sporting activity that was to make him famous throughout the world. It is said that his passion for long distance running was first kindled when the owner of the pastry shop gave him a letter to post. Pietri promptly disappeared for four hours, and on his return explained that he had delivered the letter by hand himself by running a round distance of some fifty kilometres! (*Sportstar* March 4th 2006)

He joined the local La Patria sports club and within two years he was running competitively and doing well. In 1904 he entered his first official 3000 metres race and came second. He participated in the Italian athletic championships in 1905 and won the 25 kilometre title. In 1905 he went on to win his first international marathon of 30 kilometres in Paris by nearly six minutes from the runner-up, the Frenchman Bonheure, the previous year's winner. The news of Pietri's success made him a hero in his home town and the man to watch.

Pietri's achievements attracted the interest of Mario Luigi Milne, president of the Italian Walking Union. He took him under his wing and arranged for Pietri to be assigned to an infantry regiment for two years to complete his military service. He was based at Turin, and given time to train on the local roads and to compete successfully for his regiment.

For the Athens interim Games Pietri was selected for the marathon after winning a preliminary event held in Rome. The Athens marathon was held on a very hot day in May over a distance of nearly 42 kilometres. More than thirty competitors from fifteen countries took part. Pietri ran strongly and was in the lead at the twenty-four kilometre stage when he suffered bad abdominal pains and was forced to retire.

In his last year of military service Pietri competed little in international races since he was given limited permission to run outside Turin. He reached the rank of corporal, before in September 1907 returning to civilian life. He was soon competing widely again and became the undisputed leader of Italian long distance running. In the run-up to the London Olympics he was successful in several competitions, apart from a disappointment in the Italian national marathon in which he had to retire from sunstroke after the thirty-three kilometre mark.

However, his place in the Italian Olympic team was assured, and in July Pietri left Carpi to join the rest of the team in Turin for their journey to London. On the afternoon of July 24th the little Italian runner in white T-shirt and scarlet shorts, with the number nineteen on his chest, lined up in a field of fifty-five for the start of the marathon race that was to astonish the world and make him a superstar overnight.

The story of the marathon has been described earlier but the gripping account Pietri gave to Italian journalists a few days after the race is worth relating:

"When we left Windsor I did not change my steady pace but waited until the race settled down. I was in the group with my two trainers Lunghi and Brocca who rode on bicycles. After a while I caught up with the two English runners Price and Lord and stayed with them until around the fifteen kilometre mark. I did not try to pass them for they told me that the Indian runner, Longboat, who many considered to be the probable winner, was ahead, and also that another runner was going quickly. It was Hefferon, the South African who seemed to be in magnificent shape. I thought that if he kept that up, then he is sure to win. But I did not want to chase after him. But Lord and Price thought otherwise and tried to catch up with Hefferon who still set a phenomenal pace.

"But it was fatal to them and they became exhausted. At eighteen kilometres some cyclists told us that Longboat was weakening, 'We must catch him up'. Lunghi and Brocca encouraged me. We caught the Longboat group up. He stopped for a drink and we overtook him and passed them but the trainers of Longboat urged him on and he overtook me. Their cycles caught my legs and weakened me. My trainer lost his patience and swore at them to take care. Then one of Longboat's trainers returned with a bottle of champagne. Brocca said to me, 'It must happen, that is fatal in the race.' We reached Longboat and he drank and gargled. His trainers urged him to 'Go on, Go on,' but he did not want to know and remained on the ground.

"I needed to know who was behind. So Lunghi went back and when he returned, he said it was Hayes, but the distance was two miles.

"There was a loud bang which made everybody shudder, and then a shout – 'Hefferon has entered the stadium!' But no! The race officials told us that

Hefferon was slowing down. I sped up instinctively. At four kilometres from home, Hefferon had no more than two hundred metres lead on me. The crowd urged me on. I heard them but did not see them.

"I caught him up. He looked drunk, just like Longboat. He had drunk the fatal one champagne. As I passed him he gave me a long and sad look and then stretched to the ground ... now we were first. I could have slowed down but everyone urged me to hurry. We passed between two lines of spectators. I tried to keep straight but the road made a lot of turns. Suddenly, after another bend, my heart gave a jump. I saw in front of me a grey mass and a bridge with flags. It was the stadium. And then I remembered no more" (*Athleticanet Netizie*).

In fact, on the day after the race Pietri claimed he had a little clearer impression of the final dramatic events on the stadium track. He told the *Evening News*, "Oh, the joy when I came to the tape, and found that I had won the race! I forgot all my sufferings, and was content. It was a victory for my country and myself, and I felt supremely happy, although nearly dead with exhaustion."

Interestingly, Pietri in his own reflections on the race makes no allusions to taking any refreshments from spectators, or to the claim that he was given a syringe of strychnine when he collapsed just before entering the stadium.

Johnny Hayes is now the forgotten hero of the London Marathon. He was born in New York

City in April 1886, just one year after his great rival across the Atlantic. He was of Irish stock, his mother and father having emigrated from Nenagh in Co Tipperary. His father was a baker who ran a business in Manhattan.

Hayes was a bright lad with a winning personality. He left school when he was seventeen and went to work as messenger and odd job boy at the famous Bloomingdales store. He started running when young, joined the St Bartholomew's Athletic Club of New York, and set his heart on becoming a champion long distance runner. He was what was termed "a good little 'un", only five foot three inches tall and weighing just less than nine stones. The *New York Sun* described him as "a slim, little nickeled steel athlete from his toes to the crown of his head."

Hayes enjoyed pointing out that his legs, barely thirty inches long, were what Abraham Lincoln had said were ideal for a soldier (Schaab – *An Illustrated History of the Olympics*).

In 1906 he ran for the first time in the famous Boston Marathon against a field of one hundred and finished a credible fifth in 2 hours 55 min. He competed again in the following year and improved on his performance by coming third in a time of 2 hours and 30 min. The winner of that race was Tom Longboat, who thus became one of the favourites to win the London Olympic marathon.

Later in 1907, Hayes won the first major marathon over the hilly Yonkers course in New York. After this race he was recruited to the Irish-American Athletic Club, and did not compete again until the American Olympic trials. Hayes was a strong favourite in the trial marathon, but was surprisingly beaten into second place by Thomas Morrissey, another American runner strongly fancied to do well at the London Games.

At the age of twenty-one, Hayes had however secured his place in the American team. He had tons of confidence and prepared himself meticulously for the marathon. "I just know I'm going to win," he told friends, "and I wish it were fifty miles instead of twenty-six. The next time you fellows see me I'll be wearing the laurel wreath" (*New York Times*).

He did not smoke, and drank only in moderation. He made sure he rested for two days in bed before the start of the event. On the day of the race he had a light lunch consisting of two ounces of beef, two slices of toast and a cup of tea. He took nothing to eat or drink during the actual race, believing that to do so would be a great mistake, and "merely bathed my face with Florida water and gargled my throat with brandy". (Mallon and Buchanan – *The 1908 Olympic Games*).

His running plan was equally meticulous. He knew the strength of his competitors but was determined to run his own race in London. Running in the number twenty-six, all went according to plan. With the help of the other American runners, Hayes paced himself carefully during the early stages of the race at a rate of six minutes a mile and refused to be ruffled by the fast pace being set by the leaders.

Longboat dropped out at the twenty mile mark, and Hayes, having conserved his energy, passed the South African Hefferon near to the finish, but said that he saw nothing of Pietri until he entered the stadium.

Some hours later, following the official United States protest against the assistance Pietri had received, the little Italian was disqualified and Hayes was awarded the gold medal. Late that night Hayes stayed up late sipping a beer with a friend whilst congratulations poured in. "Heat," he explained later, "never bothered me, my grandfather and father were bakers and I worked in the bakery as a boy. I was used to heat" (Schaap – *An Illustrated History of the Olympics*).

The following day he visited the House of Commons where he shook hands with members and was congratulated on his fine performance. He walked around rather stiffly but assured members that although rather footsore, he was otherwise well.

Hayes' victory was greeted enthusiastically with celebrations throughout the United States. The New York newspapers were delirious, offering "biographies of him which seemed to precede a candidacy for sainthood" (Schaefer – *The Irish American Athletic Club*). The Irish American community in particular were rightly proud of his success and that of other members of the Irish

American Club, and took full advantage to promote their own cultural identity and aspirations. Pictures appeared in the newspapers of Hayes proudly dressed in his club uniform, and the *New York Sun* underlined that "Jack Hayes is as Irish as you find them, with black hair, blue eyes, a good humoured and freckled face and a ton of confidence in himself".

Bloomingdales also jumped on to the bandwagon. When Hayes returned to New York he was surprised to see the store plastered with his photograph and had proudly proclaimed that its favourite clerk had prepared for the marathon by training on the store roof during his lunchtime and evening. It announced that it was promoting Hayes forthwith from shipping clerk to be head of the sports department. For several years sports writers went along with this account until Hayes himself admitted that it was mostly fabrication.

The truth of the matter was that Mr Bloomingdale himself had spotted Hayes' talent some time earlier, and agreed with the Irish American Club that his store would support Hayes financially to train on a track outside Manhattan (Schaap – *An Illustrated History of the Olympics*).

Had this disclosure been known at the time, it would surely have led to further controversy, and probably the disqualification of Hayes, since the rules on amateurism at that time, at least on paper, were very strict.

The sensational scenes at the end of the London marathon set off a marathon craze which excited crowds around the world, and no more so than in the United States. Once the Olympics were over, both Pietri and Hayes were offered very good money by New York promoters to turn professional and to take part in a series of elimination races leading to what was billed to be the championship of the world. Both young men needed little persuasion to accept the offer.

In the championship, they ran two races against one another. Their first was over two hundred and sixty laps on an indoor track at Madison Square Garden in New York in November 1908 in front of a large crowd. The occasion was extraordinarily rumbustious, fired by ten dollar ticket prices, heavy betting and a near riot over the final laps! The race was again close, but this time Pietri avenged his Olympic defeat by beating Hayes by around seventy yards. They competed again in March of the following year, and once more Pietri was the winner.

Over the next few years both runners took part in many more marathon races in various places in the world, usually before large and enthusiastic crowds. Pietri was particularly prolific, and in the space of five months competed in twenty-two races between ten kilometres and the marathon distance, winning seventeen of them. In Argentina it is said that he even competed against a horse. Each enjoyed their fame and both earned a lot of money.

The former pastry cook from Carpi and the clerk from Bloomingdales had come a long way.

Dorando Pietri ran his last marathon in Buenos Aires in May 1910 at the age of twenty-five, where he achieved his personal best time of 2 hrs and 38 min. It is estimated that in his three years as a professional runner he had earned two hundred thousand lira (well over £2,000) in prize money, a very large sum of money for those days. However, his business ventures were far less successful. He invested heavily in a hotel which failed, and his wayward brother subsequently ran off with much of his money. His fame forgotten, he lived out his last few years by driving a taxi.

In 1909 he had married Teresa Dondi from Carpi. The couple had no children. In his younger years Pietri had suffered from heart trouble and he died from a heart attack in 1942 at the age of fifty-six in Sanremo.

He is still revered in Italy and on July 24th 2008, the centenary of the London marathon, a statue of Dorando Pietri more than three metres high is to be raised in his home town of Carpi.

Johnny Hayes' subsequent career was somewhat more fortunate. He toured America and Europe giving exhibitions of long distance running, and earning good money. He ran no more races after 1910. He married and was appointed coach to the 1912 American Olympic team and for a number of years wrote sporting articles for the *Hudson Despatch*. He lost money in the depression years but in later life be became a successful food broker in New York. He died in Englewood, New Jersey in 1965, at the age of seventy-nine. In Ireland his achievements as an athlete are commemorated in Nenagh by a life-sized bronze statue of him and two other Irish Olympians who can trace their heritage there.

Chapter 15

Everything a runner should be
Tom Longboat

"Tom Longboat was one of the greatest athletes Canada has ever seen" – Bruce Kidd, Commonwealth Games champion, 1964.

He was a great marathon runner. Some judge that he was even the finest long distance runner of all time. In less than two months Tom Longboat won three indoor marathons. He was a superstar, and became the first professional marathon champion of the world. Yet perhaps no athlete has ever been acclaimed and defamed as much as Longboat.

Thomas Charles Longboat was born on the Six Nations Reserve near Ontario in June 1887. He was a member of the Onondaga Nation. His Indian name was Cogwagee, which means "Everything." He grew up on a small farm and helped with the ploughing, harvesting and the care of the animals. The farm was poor and the work was hard, especially after his father died when he was only five. But he had abundant energy and still found time to play lacrosse, and to chase with his brother across the reserve and into the neighbouring countryside.

His formal education came to an end when he was twelve. He worked on farms as a casual labourer and during his travels he developed a passion for running. Slim, and with long lean legs, he was every inch the athlete. He ran his first competitive race in the spring of 1905 when at seventeen he competed in the annual Victoria Day five mile race in Caledonia.

Although he did not win, he led for most of the way and was beaten only in the last mile into second place. The experience inspired him to take running seriously and improve his strength and endurance. The story goes that he trained by running to neighbouring towns so far away, and so fast, that his family did not believe him. To remove all doubt, Longboat waited until his brother was driving a horse and buggy to the neighbouring town of Hamilton, a distance of around thirty kilometres, gave him a half-hour start, and then set off on foot to beat the buggy to the town!

Still a complete unknown, he entered the Around the Bay marathon in Hamilton in 1906, a distance of some nineteen miles. Hamilton was the centre of Canadian road running and the marathon was its most important race. The favourite was an Englishman, John Marsh, who had set several English records before emigrating to Canada. Few had heard of Longboat and the betting odds against him winning the race were set at 100-1.

But his hard training had paid off and he won by almost three minutes ahead of the next runner in a time of just over 1 hour 49 mins. Winning the race made him an instant celebrity, and he followed up his success by winning other long distance races in Canada in the same year. He had proved his exceptional ability. "Longboat Always Wins", boasted the *Toronto Globe* to its Christmas readers (Kidd – *Tom Longboat*).

His next ambition was to win the race which was, and still is, one of the greatest running events in the world, the annual Boston marathon. Longboat was a firm favourite for the race and his backers had trouble placing their bets. An estimated one hundred thousand spectators lined the course and Longboat lived up to expectations. After around two-thirds of the race he suddenly sprinted into the lead, and despite the cheering spectators crowding on to the roads and slowing him down, he won the event in the very fast time of 2 hours 24 mins, beating the previous record by five minutes.

Two Americans, Bob Fowler and Johnny Hayes, finished second and third. While other runners struggled towards the finishing line, Longboat collected his victory trophy, the three-foot high statue of Mercury, and enjoyed a victory feast of chicken broth and steak.

Longboat enjoyed his newly-won fame, too much so, for shortly afterwards he was expelled from the YMCA for breaking a curfew. But he was relieved to be free of the YMCA's restrictive training rules regarding alcohol and women, and applied to join the Irish Canadian Athletic Club managed by the flamboyant former hammer thrower, Tom Flanagan. He was reluctant at first to accept Longboat – "he is a hard man to handle and we could not give him the attention he requires" – but subsequently relented, and Longboat thereafter competed in the orange and green of the Irish Canadians (Blaikie – www.davidblaikie.com – *The Canadian Story*).

Flanagan never stopped his athletes from enjoying a drink or two, or enjoying the company of women, and his more relaxed regime suited Longboat, who continued to run successfully in several races.

Flanagan was an out and out entrepreneur and favoured professional sport. He managed several professional athletes. Ideally, he would have liked to see Longboat turn professional quickly but the London Olympics were less than a year away and his protégé clearly had good chances of winning. No one knows what terms came to be agreed between him and Longboat, but it was at this time that accusations began to be made that Longboat had violated his amateur status by living like a professional in a hotel owned by Flanagan.

Flanagan hastily tried to defuse the situation by finding a cigar store for Longboat to manage and thereby demonstrate his financial independence, but the venture was short-lived since Longboat was certainly no businessman. The joke in running circles was that with few sales he had smoked most of the stock himself! (Blaike – www.davidblaikie. com – *The Canadian Story*).

Unfortunately, his amateur status had been badly damaged, especially in the eyes of Americans, and the New England Athletic Union formally declared him a professional.

Flanagan, however, was able to convince the Canadian inquiry into the affair that Longboat had broken no rules, and on the basis of his outstanding performances Longboat was selected to run in the Canadian marathon team at the Olympics. He carried the hopes of his nation.

In the weeks before the London Olympics, the Canadian press were given daily reports on his preparatory training in Ireland. His personality and unusual background made him a popular figure, and when he finally arrived in London, he was welcomed warmly everywhere. "Longboat, Fit as a Fiddle, and Idolised by the British Public" was the headline in the *Toronto Daily Star*.

He went into the marathon as one of the strong favourites, and his subsequent failure to complete the course dismayed his supporters and his country. On that hot and humid day, he ran well early on and was well placed before collapsing without warning at the twenty mile mark. He staggered to his feet and tried to continue, but was forced into a nearby car by medical officials. His followers were dumbfounded and when the news was flashed to the White City Stadium the humiliated Canadians had to endure the mirth of the crowd.

The post-mortems carried out by the Canadian camp were front page news in the Canadian papers.

Longboat said that he had been struck by a sudden weakness and dropped like a log. Some people suggested that he had over-trained. But other more sinister rumours grew that he had been drugged, even perhaps by his own manger, Flanagan, for his own ends, perhaps even as a betting coup. Although doubts remained, the charge of any corruption was never substantiated. The incident was, concluded the *Hamilton Spectator*, "just one more incident in an athletic event that ran the gladiatorial games of ancient Rome a good second".

Hugely disappointed, Longboat announced his retirement. Flanagan, however, quickly made him change his mind, and the Canadian was soon once more winning important races and setting national records. In the autumn of 1906 he won his third straight Ward Marathon title. It was his last race as an amateur. Lured by the promise of huge prizes he turned professional.

After the London Olympics, two New York promoters took full advantage of the massive publicity coverage that followed the London marathon by organising what was billed as the World Professional Marathon Championship. They signed up Dorando Pietri and Johnny Hayes to race against one another, and they invited Longboat to run against the winner. The winner of that race would then have to compete against the highly-regarded English professional runner, Alf Shrubb, to decide the championship.

As described earlier Pietri won the rematch

against Hayes, and his race against Longboat took place at the Madison Square Garden in New York in December 1906. The winner's prize was $3000 with $2000 for the loser.

It was to prove yet another sensational marathon and the public loved it. Pietri had already found in his race against Hayes that indoor running ideally suited his way of running and set off at a relentless pace. However, he was unable to shake off the dogged Longboat. At nineteen miles Pietri suddenly veered off the track and collapsed into the arms of his brother, Ulpiano. The Canadian, although near to exhaustion himself and with badly blistered feet, staggered on over the remaining miles to finish the race and so prevent any disputes over winning bets. In Canada news of his victory caused huge excitement. "Bring on your next champion", *The Globe* boasted "Longboat is undoubtedly the fastest long distance man in the world".

The final race between Longboat and Alf Shrubb was set to be held on February 5th 1909, also at the Madison Square Garden. The English runner Shrubb had been a professional since 1906, and although he had never before completed the full marathon distance, he was an outstanding distance runner. Longboat needed to beat him to be truly recognised as the world champion. However, rumours began to circulate about the Canadian's physical condition and his attitude to training. Flanagan made matters worse by selling his contract with Longboat to another New York promoter for

$2000, claiming that his charge would not follow his strict training programme. Longboat, upset by the suddenness of the move, later complained bitterly that "he sold me just like a race horse to make money" (Blaikie – www.davidblaikie.com – *The Canadian Story*).

The race was held at nine o'clock in the evening before a standing and boisterous crowd of twelve thousand who had to be held back from the track by a line of policemen. The first half of the race belonged clearly to Shrubb who by twenty-four kilometres was a good eight laps ahead of Longboat. The crowd began to turn against the Canadian and even booed. But Longboat had run a sensible race and he gradually hauled in the Englishman. Excitement grew. At thirty-two kilometres he had reduced the margin to six laps. Then, with less than two miles to go, he caught and swept past Shrubb to the acclaim of the screaming spectators. The exhausted Englishman left the track. Longboat coasted to victory, amidst what was reported to be the greatest excitement that ever marked a contest at the Garden stadium. Longboat was declared the professional champion of the world.

Tom Longboat continued to race until 1913, not only in North America but also in Britain where he ran at Powderhall in Scotland. Several of his races involved his old rivals such as Pietri and Shrubb, and he was not always successful. But whatever the race, he was always a battler, and the crowds loved him for it and flocked to see him. In his first three seasons as a professional it is estimated that he earned about $17,000, a substantial sum at that time.

He was not always successful, and when he lost he continued to face those accusations of being a lazy Indian and a runner not prepared to train hard enough. When he received a suspended sentence for drunkenness in Toronto, he was even accused of being an alcoholic. Longboat, always a generous man, enjoyed celebrating his success with his friends and sharing a drink with them, but there is no hard evidence that it was anything more than that.

The outbreak of the First World War spelt the end of professional racing as a popular spectacle and Longboat volunteered for the Army in 1916. He served in France and found time to compete in races against other Allied troops. As a despatch runner he was assigned to carry messages from one battlefield post to another. In the mud, wire and craters around Vimy and Passchendaele, this was dangerous work. He was wounded twice and once reported dead after a shell buried him in a communications trench. He was demobilised in 1919.

When he returned home, he found that not only had his wife, Lauretta, remarried but the interest of the public in matched prize races had virtually gone. Unemployed, he sought work wherever he could find it. Times were hard and he pawned his medals to make ends meet. Eventually, when he was forty, he found permanent work in the streets department of the City of Toronto where for the most part he collected rubbish.

He worked there quietly and dependably for twenty years before retiring to his beloved Six Nations Reserve where he died from pneumonia in 1949 at the age of sixty-one. He was buried in accordance with his traditional Indian faith, and the service was conducted entirely in Onondaga. Many people from the sporting world gathered there to pay their respects, including his fellow Canadian Bill Sherring who had won the 1906 Athens marathon.

Tom Longboat's greatness as an athlete is now fully recognised. He has been placed in the Canadian Aboriginal Hall of Fame, and also in the Canadian Sports Hall of Fame. His name remains an inspiration to all athletes, and each year the Tom Longboat Awards are presented to the top Aboriginal amateur runners in Canada.

Chapter 16

From "dirty water" to Olympic gold
Henry Taylor

"Henry Taylor, a twenty-three-year-old Englishman, emerged as the first authentic swimming star of the Olympics." – Dick Schaap, sports historian.

Henry Taylor deserves his accolade as Britain's greatest amateur swimmer. He dominated British middle distance swimming in the early 1900s. He won three gold medals for Great Britain at the 1908 Games. In total, he competed at four Olympic Games and won eight medals, more than any other British competitor in the history of the Olympics.

He was born in 1885 at Hollinwood, Oldham, to James and Elizabeth Taylor. His father was a coal miner. He was orphaned at an early age and was brought up by his elder brother, William. His upbringing was hard and he was poorly educated. He was a popular and cheerful lad. When he left school, he went to work in the local cotton mill.

Taylor learnt to swim in the local Hollinwood Canal and swam at the central baths in Oldham on the so-called "dirty water" days when the admission charges were reduced. He swam his first race at the baths aged seven. It was a two-length race for boys which he won and received a silver medal. His success inspired his love for the sport and he joined the local Chadderton swimming club. His brother acted as his trainer, but he spent a lot of time training alone in open water in the Hollinwood Canal during his lunch breaks, and then in the Alexandra Boating Lake in Oldham in the evening. The way he resolutely ploughed his path through the boats on the lake made him a popular spectacle.

By his early twenties, competing for the Chadderton Swimming Club, he had proved himself to be a formidable distance swimmer though he had not yet won any major championship. He was a stocky man, five foot five inches, and, at his best, around ten-and-a-half stone. His particular strength was the so-called "trudgen" stroke, a double over-arm stroke requiring considerable upper body strength and stamina, and which generated a very powerful drive from a most effective scissor kick.

His first major swimming success was in the interim 1906 Olympic Games in Athens. He went to the Games as a travelling reserve and his success was a major surprise since he had not had the benefit of proper training facilities. However, the swimming events were held in the open sea at Phalerum Bay and the waves could be very rough at times, making it difficult for the swimmers to breathe.

The organisation was also poor. No one seemed to know when the next race would take place and the judges had difficulty in keeping the swimming lanes free from private boats. Taylor's experience of all those hours of swimming in Alexandra Park served him well and he seemed to thrive in the conditions.

He mastered the waves, and went on to win the gold medal for the 1 mile swim in a time of 28 min 28 sec, nearly two minutes ahead of his nearest rival.

So determined was he to win the medal, he kept his head firmly down in the last stages of the race and swam further than the actual distance! He followed up his success at Athens by winning a silver medal for the 400 metres and a bronze in the 4x200 metres relay race.

The 1908 London Games were the scene of Henry Taylor's greatest triumph. The swimming events were held in a 100 metre pool for the first time. He won individual gold medals in the 1500 metres and the 400 metres, as well as a gold for his part in the victorious British 4x200 metres relay team. In both the 400 and 1500 metre races he established the first official world records.

Taylor's performance in the relay was equally remarkable. Swimming the anchor leg, he entered the water three yards down on the American, Rich, and ten behind the powerful Hungarian swimmer, Halmay. Showing great determination, Taylor caught up with Rich fifty yards from home. It still seemed probable that the Hungarian would win, but he was swimming erratically and suffering from cramp. Suddenly he veered across the course and struck the side of the pool. Taylor powered on to pass and win by five yards. Halmay, who had lost consciousness, had to be hauled from the pool before he drowned.

Taylor returned home to Lancashire in triumph to a tumultuous reception. He competed again for Great Britain in the 1912 and 1920 Olympiads held in Stockholm and Antwerp respectively but not quite so successfully.

By then the American swimmers had perfected the new front crawl stroke for middle distance swimming which was faster than the trudgen. Nevertheless, Taylor still won a bronze medal in the 4x200 metres relay at both events. If war had not forced the cancellation of the 1916 Games he would have surely added to this tally.

Back at home he dominated swimming competitions for several years. The famous Morecambe Bay race was one of his favourite competitions. He swam the 13 mile race for twenty years, winning it from 1910 to 1914, and four more times after the war.

In 1914 he had swum across the bay in just over two hours, a time so fast that cynics accused him of running over sandbanks! His winning times will never be bettered as the course has been altered considerably over the years.

During World War I, Taylor served in the Royal

Navy as an able seaman and was soon acknowledged as the Navy's champion swimmer. To achieve this distinction he had to swim around the British fleet at anchorage at Scapa Flow, which he repeated on a number of occasions. Given the size of the fleet at that time, and the temperature of the sea, this was an extraordinary exploit. Much less known is Henry Taylor's reputation as something of a war hero. In the Battle of Jutland in 1916 his ship was sunk, and he and others of the ship's company were in the sea for two hours before being rescued. Apparently, Henry Taylor swam around his fellow shipmates urging them to keep afloat, and encouraging them not to despair (www.chadderton-hs.freeuk.com).

He retired from swimming in 1926. He was a handsome man but, reportedly, as a young man, "he was never allowed near the ladies", because his brother felt it would interfere with his training. (*Oldham Evening Chronicle*). He remained a bachelor all his life. Lacking a formal education, he found life difficult in his later years.

He mortgaged his thirty-five trophies and more than three hundred medals to buy a pub but it was not a success, and he never redeemed them. Unemployed for several years, the local council eventually found him a post as an attendant at Chadderton swimming baths where he had spent many hours as a boy and young man.

A quiet man, he never boasted about his achievements at the Olympic Games. He died at his home just behind the Chadderton Baths in October

1951 at the age of sixty-five. In 1969 his memory was honoured at the Swimming Hall of Fame in Florida. In England, a blue plaque was unveiled to this great but neglected swimmer at the sports centre in Chadderton in 2002.

Chapter 17

Skating Pioneer
Madge Syers

"The wonderful accuracy of her figures, combined with perfect carriage and movement, was the chief feature of the morning's skating." – Olympic 1908 Official Report.

Florence Madeline Syers (née Cave), best known as Madge Syers, was a British ice-skater. She was the first woman to compete at the highest level in her sport and became the first women to be a world and Olympic figure skating champion. A pioneer in her sport, she created a sensation when she competed as the only woman in the 1902 World Ice Skating Championships which had hitherto been a male preserve, and took the second place.

She was born in Kensington, London, in 1881, the fourth daughter in the family of fifteen children of Edward and Elizabeth Cave. Her father, who traded in hosiery and speculated in property development, lived extravagantly and eventually became bankrupt. Little else is known about Syers' childhood but her interest in sport must have been encouraged since as well as skating she was a gifted swimmer and equestrienne. The fashionable Prince's Club ice rink in Knightsbridge was near her home and it was there that she soon demonstrated her exceptional skating ability. She was said to excel at the comparatively restrictive style favoured by English skaters at that time. When she was eighteen she had her first real success by winning the challenge shield in a team event. Shortly afterwards, she met her future husband, Edgar Syers, described as "a gentleman of independent means" (Dictionary of National Biography), and they began to skate and compete together.

Edgar Syers was eighteen years older than Madge and as a coach he was to have a significant influence on his wife's skating development. He favoured the more artistic and athletic skating technique popular abroad and encouraged Syers to abandon the rigid English style for one that was much more ambitious and more physically demanding. Growing in confidence, Syers also started a fashion trend by wearing shorter length skirts and bright and fashionable clothing. In 1899 the couple won the first British pairs skating competition, and early in 1900 they had their first international success when they came second to an Austrian couple in Berlin. They married later in the year.

In 1902 Syers took the initiative that was to startle the ice skating establishment when she submitted her entry to compete in the world figure skating championships organised by the

International Skating Union (ISU) in London. Syers had discovered that there was nothing in their rule book prohibiting women ice skaters competing against men since it had never occurred to the ISU that women would even try.

Skating in a smart woollen skirt, satin blouse, gloves and pearls, she gave a very attractive and stirring performance, and finished second in the competition to the defending Swedish champion, Ulrich Salchow. The *Manchester Guardian* reported that "Mrs Syers is without doubt the finest woman skater in England, and can have few rivals abroad even".

Indeed many observers thought Syers deserved to have won, and Ulrich is said to have taken off his medal and given it to her (www.skatefic.com).

After Syers' success, the ISU closed the loophole and passed a rule prohibiting women skaters from competing against men, ostensibly on the grounds that the long skirts of the women skaters made it difficult for the judges to see their feet. However, owing to a technicality, the rule could not be implemented immediately and the defiant Syers in 1903 entered and won the first British single championships. Further successes in open competitions followed, and forced the ISU to concede that women skaters could be as proficient as men.

In 1905 the ban was lifted, and by the following year a separate ladies' event had been introduced at the world championships in Davos. Syers entered the championships and won, and repeated her victory again in 1907 in Vienna.

She now set her sights on the 1908 Olympics in which figure skating events were to be held for the first time. The event took place at the end of October at the rink where her career had begun – the Princes Club in Knightsbridge. The rink was full with enthusiastic spectators. In the compulsory figures and free skating she was placed first by all five judges and thus became the first woman Olympic champion in the sport.

The Times reported that in the compulsory figures Syers was the chief feature of the morning's skating, and that "she had never given a better performance; its essential power was concealed by the ease of execution." In the free skating she had excelled; she skated without a fault, "with her own particular dash and finish", Syers also achieved a unique double by winning a bronze medal with Edgar in the pairs event.

Unfortunately, Madge Syers never competed again. Soon after the Olympics her health began to fail and she retired from skating. In September 1917 she died of heart failure at her home in Weybridge at the age of thirty-five. She was a great skater who loved her sport. She once wrote, "Skating is an exercise fitted for both old and young. It may be taken as an exacting art or merely as a pleasant diversion. Its difficulties make it all the more interesting. There are always new fields to conquer."

In 1981 Madge Syers was inducted into the World Ice Skating Hall Of Fame, the highest honour a figure skater can attain.

Chapter 18

From Sydney to Hollywood
Snowy Baker

"He tried everything, and invariably succeeded at everything, proving the virtues of a busy lifestyle." – Greg Growden, author and sports writer.

Reginald Leslie "Snowy" Baker has the reputation of being the finest all round sportsman ever seen in Australia, and his life has a film star quality about it, fitting for a man who spent some years working in Hollywood.

It is estimated that during his lifetime he competed to a high standard in well over twenty different sports as diverse as fencing, wrestling, swimming, polo and rugby. Although he did not actually win a gold medal, he remains the only Australian to have represented his country in three different sports at the Olympic Games. A man of great drive and energy, his post Olympic career was equally famous as a Hollywood stuntman, boxing promoter, writer, actor and film maker. And yet he was scorned by some as being something of a spiv, a man too full of himself and a dodgy boxing promoter and businessman. Some of his countrymen never forgave him for his part in the rise and fall of Australia's most romanticised sporting figure, the boxer Les Darcy.

He was born in Sydney in 1884, the son of George Baker, an Irish-born council clerk, and his wife Elizabeth. Very blond, it was inevitable that from an early age he would be called "Snowy". He was a very lively and energetic boy, and his sporting father encouraged him to be as versatile as possible. He learned horsemanship at early morning rides at the local race course.

He quickly became an exceptional swimmer, unbeatable amongst those of his age. He won several swimming championships for his school and played water polo for the East Sydney Swimming Club. His speed, strength and endurance made him an exceptional half back in rugby union and when he was twenty he represented New South Wales against both Queensland and the Great Britain touring side of 1904.

His reputation as a "rare tackler ... and as hard a player for his weight as has been seen in the game" (Australian Dictionary of Biography) earned him a cap for Australia in the first test against Great Britain. He was also a talented rower and cricketer.

As a young man he joined the New South Wales Lancers regiment which offered a strong sporting side to its military activities. Snowy thrived in its well-organised programme of tournaments involving a wide range of sports. He became a sergeant and won prizes in a variety of sports such as fencing, wrestling on horseback, rifle shooting and tent-pegging. But the most important was boxing, which he took up seriously when he was eighteen. In 1905 he had progressed to become the amateur middleweight champion of both New South Wales and Victoria, and in the following year won also the heavyweight boxing title of Australia.

When he was invited to compete in the 1907 Amateur Boxing Association (ABA) Championships in London, Baker jumped at the chance to earn an international reputation. His high hopes of success were destroyed by ill health.

Apparently, while with friends at a bar in Port Said, he declined to join them in a round of whisky and opted instead for two glasses of water. This was a bad mistake. For the rest of the voyage he felt off colour, and shortly after his arrival in England in February 1907 he became deliriously ill with enteric fever which was nearly to cost him his life.

He missed out on the ABA championships and recuperated in Ireland to build up his strength. It was not long before he was receiving invitations to take part in swimming and diving events and exhibitions in Britain and in Europe. His performances became very popular and crowds, it was said, flocked to see him "clamber up the most rickety of diving towers, before performing flips, dives and leaps into specially constructed pools, or the ocean" (Growden – *The Snowy Baker Story*).

He had planned to take part in the ABA championships in the following year but once more illness spoilt his chances. He contracted pneumonia and, bitterly disappointed, made plans to return home after he had recovered. Out of the blue, he received an invitation to represent Australia in the 1908 Olympics not only in the boxing, but in both the swimming and diving competitions. Happily, the swimming and diving events were scheduled for July as part of the summer Games and the boxing later in October, but given his recent ill-health, Snowy still faced a very demanding prospect.

At the swimming, he was a member of the Australian 4x200 metre freestyle relay team which finished fourth. This was the event that Britain won largely through Henry Taylor's mighty efforts. In the springboard diving, bold and exciting as he was, Baker lacked the degree of technical ability to impress the judges and lost in the first round. But he now had the time to concentrate on his main Olympic goal – the middleweight boxing title.

He certainly needed all the strength he could summon, for on the day of the event he faced a most onerous schedule. To reach the final he had to survive three preliminary bouts in the space of eleven hours. He made an instant impression and was the only foreign competitor to win a bout. He won his three preliminary fights, two of them by knockouts, and took his place in the final.

His opponent in the final was the English boxer, JWHT Douglas, known derisively in Australia as

"Johnny Won't Hit Today." Douglas had earned his nickname as a dour, ruthless and stonewalling batsman. He was nonetheless one of the best and fittest cricketers of his day and later captained England on a Test tour of Australia.

He certainly looked more like a boxer than a cricketer, and so grim that some argued that he was worth watching only when he stepped into the ring. Well before the competition started, Douglas had realised that Snowy would be his most formidable opponent and planned carefully for the eventuality, even to the extent of having his scouts watch Snowy's training sessions.

In an epic final he beat Baker on points in a fierce bout which soon had the crowd on its feet. The official report described how "the exchanges were of a heavy order before Douglas lifted his adversary clean off his feet with a blow to the jaw." The points were so close that the judges had considerable difficulty in reaching a decision.

This gave rise to the popular myth, which is still repeated today, that the fight was finally left to the decision of the referee, who happened to be Douglas' father. In fact his father was not the referee, and was at the ringside only to present the medals in his capacity as president of the ABA. Douglas' victory was by a very narrow margin of points. The official report of the Olympiad concluded that Snowy was one of the best amateur performers ever seen in a ring, but the "verdict rightly went to the Englishman".

Another legend that became popular soon after the Olympics was that Baker and Douglas were persuaded to have a bare knuckle fight at London's prestigious National Sporting Club and this time Baker knocked out Douglas in the second round. However, attractive as it might sound, there is no evidence to support the story.

On his return to Australia in 1908, Baker was given a rapturous welcome in Sydney and wasted no time on building on his success. He had considerable business acumen. He opened a physical culture establishment which began marketing mail order courses. Snowy soon branched out into journalism.

He contributed articles to the *Sydney Evening News*, and in 1912 launched his own penny monthly publication called *Snowy Baker's Magazine*, in which he used to promote his own health theories and products. It covered advice on matters ranging from how to become a master at jujitsu and to keep thin and acquire a graceful figure, to the fun of whaler racing and how to look after a bull terrier.

The magazine was very popular and reached a circulation of more than three thousand. In 1909 he was fortunate enough to marry, Ethel MacKay, a widow aged thirty-seven, after a whirlwind romance. Ethel shared Snowy's passion for sport, and was a practical and strong-willed woman who proved to be of enormous help to him in his career.

Boxing soon also attracted his business interest.

Working with a rather dubious entrepreneur and showman by the name of Hugh D ("Huge Deal") McIntosh he established himself as one of Australia's leading boxing promoters, and was soon successfully bringing several international boxers to Australia to fight. In 1912 Snowy bought the Rushcutters Bay Stadium in Sydney from McIntosh for £30,000 and promptly renamed it "Snowy Baker's Stadium".

It was not long before further Baker's Stadiums were established in Melbourne, Adelaide and Brisbane. In green trousers and a hat, he even refereed many bouts himself. He prided himself at spotting talented boxers, and was to play an important part in the career of the brilliant young Australian middleweight, Les Darcy.

Darcy's prowess as a boxer and his handsome features and boyish personality made him hugely popular, especially with the Catholic, Irish working class population. Snowy eventually took over the young boxer's engagements. He staged Darcy's first fight at the Sydney stadium in 1914 and steadily promoted the fighter's world championship credentials.

When World War I broke out, Darcy ran into criticism for not volunteering like other young Australians for the armed services. He was denied a passport to go to the United States to fight for the world title. He fell out with Snowy, who felt badly betrayed when Darcy stowed away on a ship to America in 1916. Snowy reacted angrily by taking sides with the patriotic press in publicly denouncing Darcy as unpatriotic and a shirker. Darcy, who had started training for the world middleweight title, was stunned by the criticism, and volunteered for the US Army. Tragically, however, his life was short-lived. He collapsed from a badly infected tooth and died from the resulting infection in May 1917, aged just twenty-one.

When the news reached Australia, Snowy found himself facing accusations that he had unfairly hounded Darcy to death in America and thus shared responsibility for the tragic end of such a promising career. He was jeered and screamed at in the street – "you're the one who killed our Les" (Growden – *The Snowy Baker Story*). Although an official inquiry cleared him of such charges, Snowy's popularity was undoubtedly badly compromised, and he could never quite shake off the allegation that somehow he was to blame for Darcy's death.

During the war years boxing in Australia lost some of its public appeal. Baker tried to boost audiences by putting on shows and vaudeville acts at his stadiums. But he soon appreciated that the best chances of success lay with the burgeoning film industry.

By 1918 he had formed his own film company, Snowy Baker Films, and started to star himself as an actor. He played a secret agent in *The Enemy Within* and a station hand in the *Lure of the Bush*. Further film appearances followed. All his roles ensured that they featured his expertise as a horse rider on his famous grey horse, Boomerang. The films were very popular and Snowy became one of Australia's first matinee idols.

In August 1920, much attracted by the prospects in America, he decided to pursue his film career there. He did appear in five Hollywood films, but though he could not act very well, his stunts were most impressive. In the *Shadow of Lightning Ridge*, Snowy leaps from the galloping Boomerang onto a train, jumps the horse through the roof of a mountain hut, rides on a narrow log around a waterfall, and then fights a guard in a horse box (Growden – *The Snowy Baker Story*).

He became very much involved with the Hollywood set and counted among his friends such stars as Charlie Chaplin, Spencer Tracy, Rudolph Valentino, Will Rogers and Shirley Temple.

In the States, he was also successful as a sports coach and businessman. As the director of the exclusive Riviera Country Club in Santa Monica, California, he tutored Hollywood stars in horse riding and other skills. It is reported he taught Valentino to kiss, Fairbanks how to use a sword and whip, and the twelve-year-old Elizabeth Taylor how to ride for the film *National Velvet*. He was himself a keen polo player and played well into the 1940s.

Snowy Baker returned to Australia in 1952 for a short time, ostensibly to explore the possibility of starting up a Riviera type club near Sydney. But he was no longer a fit and healthy man, and soon after he went back to Los Angeles he died of heart disease. At his funeral his brother, Frank, repeated Snowy Baker's last words to the crowd: "I was lucky. The good God was kind to me" (Growden – *The Snowy Baker Story*).

Chapter 19

The best and worst of Games

"They were at the beginning of one of those great world movements which was going to develop long after all present had passed away." – Rev de Courcy Laffan addressing his audience at an Olympic Banquet at the end of the London Games.

It was to be the best and worst of Games. Before London, the Olympiad had nearly died from poor organisation and the lack of popular interest. With just two years' notice, and with no financial support from the government, London prepared for, and staged in 1908, the largest, most representative and ambitious sporting spectacle that the world had ever seen.

The enormous task of drawing up the details of a complete code of Olympic rules for all the sports concerned would never have been achieved unless the executive power had been entrusted to the great British sporting associations, a principle indeed heartily approved of by James Sullivan himself. And yet for all the success, the Games were marred by disputes and controversy to such an extent that some felt they sounded the death knell of the Olympic movement rather than its revival.

First the successes. The Olympic schedule was expanded to over twenty separate sports, with each for the first time organised under its own carefully prepared regulations. Tennis was restored to the Games, and hockey and diving were introduced for the first time.

A significant step forward was taken towards the competition of women in the Olympics by introducing women's ice skating into the programme and by including gymnastics as a demonstration sport. Concepts such as national teams, entry standards and the use of preliminary heats were established which set the pattern for future Olympics. The definition of amateurism was clarified. The standard for future international swimming was set by building a 100 metre pool, clearly marked into lanes.

For the first time in the modern era the cream of the world's athletes had gathered for the Games. Never before had Great Britain taken the occasion seriously, but this time they contributed by far the largest team.

The athletic standards were high. In the competitions in and out of the stadium, there were some outstanding individual performances. Six new world records were set in the track and field competitions. In the swimming pool, all six events were won in world record times. "We have seen", concluded *The Times,* "wonderful feats of athletic skill accomplished, many of them greater than any that have been recorded in the history of the world".

And out of the dramatic events of the Games emerged the world's first sporting superstars.

But there was an undoubted downside. True, some of the problems experienced by the British organisers in the Games were not of their making. They stemmed more from some fundamental faults in the organisation behind the Olympic movement, and from the decisions that had been made earlier or had failed to be taken. The events in London exposed the International Olympic Committee as a clumsy, exclusive group of men, out of their depth in directing large scale events like the Olympics.

The IOC's decision to leave the judging of all the Games' competitions entirely in the hands of Britain as the host country proved to be a particularly costly mistake. This lesson was learned, and in subsequent Games the arrangements for the fair judging of each event has been placed firmly within an international governing body for each particular sport. No longer would it be possible for the host country to provide all the judges, officials and scorers.

Another problem, and the one that dramatically affected the 400 metres final, was the failure of the committee to put in place any means of how differences in national custom and practice arising in competition could be satisfactorily resolved. This was another issue that was forced into the limelight and sorted out after the London Games.

Other matters, too, of a more technical nature were learned from the Games. The importance of having running lanes for track events was firmly established. It was agreed in future that there would always be a planting hole and a soft landing area provided for the pole vaulters, and a stopboard for the shot putters.

However, there were also problems for which the British organisers must take most of the blame. The initial publicity about the Games had been poor and the entrance prices pitched too high, and this had badly affected attendance in the early days of the competition. The socialist American newspaper, the *New York Evening Call*, seized upon this as an indictment of the snobbishness of the English organisers to keep out "the masses of the people".

The weather was poor, and therefore the condition of the stadium arena often became treacherous, especially for the cyclists. The programme of the events in the stadium was on some days poorly planned and caused considerable confusion. The stadium at times swarmed with judges, scorers, trainers, timers, as well as the athletes.

One observer likened it to watching a three ringed circus. "At one time, a dozen cyclists were wheeling along the outer edge of the oval, while twenty runners were racing on the cinder path just inside of it. Swimmers in bright coloured caps were splashing through the long tank, whilst on the greensward members of the Danish and German gymnastic clubs, arrayed in white uniform, were performing spectacular feats on the horizontal and parallel bars" (*New York Times*, July 15th 1908).

There were issues too arising from the unhygienic condition of the swimming pool. No filtration or chlorination had been provided and the water turned into a thick pea-soup. The competitors had difficulty in seeing ahead of them, and were concerned that they might go down with some disease. Such problems succeeded in upsetting a number of foreign teams, not least the Americans, who lost no time in labelling the Games as the worst managed athletics meeting the world had yet seen.

Baron de Coubertin, too, was unhappy with aspects of the London Games, and was particularly concerned about the inexorable rise of nationalism. Nationalistic pride and fervour were nothing new and had been evident in earlier Games. When Loues won the marathon in Greece in 1896, he was rewarded by jubilant Greek patriots with large sums of money and other gifts, as well as numerous proposals of marriage.

In Paris in 1900 the Germans found their accommodation so deficient that they were convinced that their French hosts had set out deliberately to insult them. Also in Paris, foreign competitors in the marathon were convinced that the race of twenty-five miles through the Bois de Boulogne and the maze of Paris streets had been designed to allow the home town runners to take full advantage of their knowledge of the back alley ways. The race was won by a Parisian baker in a time almost three quarters of an hour faster than the hot American favourite for the race!

In London, nationalism definitely became much more institutionalised and it took on a more strident tone. It was the first Olympiad in which the competing countries were represented by national teams, and not by clubs and individuals, as had been the case hitherto. Now the athletes competed for their country, not just for themselves, and they were judged as such. The flying of national flags, the parade of the teams, the medal awards, and partisan press reports, all fuelled nationalistic feelings and emotions.

Nationalism undoubtedly played a large part in the troubles that occurred between Great Britain and the United States during and after the London Games, the so-called Battle of Shepherd's Bush. Both countries, especially though the eyes of their national press, saw in the London Games an opportunity to demonstrate their national vigour and athletic supremacy over the other.

No national team had trained harder or was better prepared for the Games than the Americans. The strong anti-British feeling of some of the Irish athletes was not necessarily shared by all the members of the team, but they all came determined that America should prove victorious. The same ambition was shared by the American officials, who were fiercely protective of their team and very ready to challenge anything that hindered its success.

The abrasive and ambitious James Sullivan was clearly a troublemaker. He seems to have concluded early on that there was a British conspiracy against the American team. He ruthlessly exploited opportunities to condemn what he saw as the stupidity and unfairness of British officials, and made good use of the American press to air his grievances. Sullivan even triggered a diplomatic incident by parading a "British Lion" in chains and on a leash at a reception for the returning American team!

There was fault, too, on the British side. The more reserved British public and press objected to the high-spirited behaviour of the American athletes and their supporters. whom they too readily branded as braggish, ill-mannered and boastful. Not for the first time at an Olympic Games, spectators took particular exception to the hoots and shouts of the American supporters, and King Edward himself was said to be upset by their "barbarous cries". The upshot was that the Americans lost the sympathy of the crowd and on occasions it was downright hostile to them.

The Americans were undoubtedly also victims of some inept and insensitive decisions by British officials, some of whom clearly flaunted their bias. For example, when the American sprinters were surprisingly beaten by the Canadian Kerr in the 200 metres, one of the judges followed him all the way into the dressing room congratulating him effusively. Moreover, it was not just their reservations about the competence and fairness of the British officials that offended the Americans.

They were also upset and irritated by the general attitude shown by some towards them, which they thought arrogant, high-handed and condescending. However, it would be wrong to conclude that the American experience was typical of the Games in general. Several countries at the end of the Games paid genuine tribute to how they had been treated by officials and benefited from their experience and special knowledge. And even the United States contingent never wavered in their friendly attitude towards Lord Desborough as the official head of the Games.

In retrospect, however, several of the disputes that took place during the London Games, though appearing serious enough at the time, now seem rather petty and even comic. Some sixty years later, the American pole vaulter, Edward Cook, who shared the gold medal in London, summed it up rather well when asked what he thought about some of the controversies at the Games. He replied, "Oh, yeah, I remember something about the flag business; I guess maybe the British did forget to fly the American flag. I don't remember why. And, yeah, I can see us now at the opening ceremonies walking into the stadium – who was that dummy who led us in? He was carrying the flag and failed to dip it. I remember that, yeah, I remember that. It was a light thing, though, nothing really" (Johnson – *All that Glitters is not Gold*).

To conclude, as the history of the Games has shown, there is always an underlying conflict between the professed idealism of the Olympic movement, and the reality of the problems and challenges that inevitably surround such a momentous event. The 1908 Olympics were no exception. Launched in a spirit of benevolent idealism, they were far from perfect and beset by controversy. But for all their troubles, they never lost their sense of dignity and have much to be proud of. They should be rightly celebrated. Important consequences flowed from them, crucial to the success of future Olympics. After 1908, the Games were firmly established as the world's premier athletic event. And the London Olympiad moreover gave the world some of the most stirring and dramatic sporting spectacles in sporting history. "Dorando's" Olympics will be forever remembered.

As London once more prepares to host the Games, a set of new and different challenges will have to be met and resolved. No doubt, like its predecessors in 1908 and 1948, it too will overcome them and leave its own distinctive legacy to the Olympic movement.

STATISTICS
1908 Olympics: Competitors by Nation

	Men	Women	Total
Argentina	1	-	1
Australia	27	-	27
Austria	7	-	7
Belgium	70	-	70
Bohemia	18	-	18
Canada	87	-	87
Denmark	78	-	78
Finland	62	-	62
France	208	-	208
Germany	79	2	81
Great Britain	697	39	736
Greece	20	-	20
Hungary	65	-	65
Iceland	1	-	1
Italy	66	-	66
The Netherlands	113	-	113
New Zealand	3	-	3
Norway	69	-	69
Russia	6	-	6
South Africa	14	-	14
Sweden	100	0	100
Switzerland	1	-	1
United States	122	-	122
Totals	1,979	44	2,023
Nations	23	3	23

Source: Mallon and Buchanan

1908 Olympics: Medals

Country	Gold	Silver	Bronze	Total
Great Britain	56	49	38	143
United States	22	12	12	46
Sweden	8	6	11	25
France	5	4	9	18
Canada	3	3	9	15
Germany	3	5	5	13
Belgium	1	5	2	8
Hungary	3	3	2	8
Norway	2	3	3	8
Denmark	0	2	3	5
Finland	1	1	3	5

Australia	1	2	1	4
Greece	0	3	1	4
Italy	2	2	0	4
Russia	1	2	0	3
Bohemia	0	0	2	2
Netherlands	0	0	2	2
South Africa	1	1	0	2
Austria	0	0	1	1
New Zealand	0	0	1	1

Source: Mallon and Buchanan

Medallists

Gold	Silver	Bronze

Archery

Men
York Round

W Dod (GBR)	R Brooks-King (GBR)	H Richardson (USA)

Continental Style

E Grisot (FRA)	L Vernet (FRA)	G Cabaret (FRA)

Women
National Round

Q Newall (GBR)	C Dod (GBR)	B Hill-Lowe (GBR)

Athletics

100m

R Walker (RSA) 10.8	J Rector (USA) 10.9	R Kerr (CAN) 11.0

200m

R Kerr (CAN) 22.6	R Cloughen (USA) 22.6	N Cartmell (USA) 22.7

400m

W Halswelle (GBR) 50.0	–	–

800m

M Sheppard (USA) 1:52.8	E Lunghi (Ita) 1:54.2	H Braun (GER) 1:55.2

1500m

M Sheppard (USA) 4:03.4	H Wilson (GBR) 4:03.6	N Hallows (GBR) 4:04.0

10,000m (Held Over 5 Miles)

E Voigt (GBR) 25:11.2	E Owen (GBR) 25:24.0	J Svanberg (SWE) 25:37.2

Marathon

J Hayes (USA) 2:55:18.4	C Hefferon (RSA) 2:56:06.0	J Forshaw (USA) 2:57:10.4

3000mS/c

A Russell (GBR) 10:47.8	A Robertson (GBR) 10:48.4	J Eisele (USA) 11:00.8

110mh

F Smithson (USA) 15.0	J Garrels (USA) 15.7	A Shaw (USA) 15.8

400mh

C Bacon (USA) 55.0	H Hillman (USA) 55.3	L Tremeer (GBR) 57.0

Medley Relay

USA 3:29.4	GER 3:32.4	HUN 3:32.5

High Jump

H Porter (USA) 1.905	C Leahy (GBR) 1.88	–
	I Somodi (Hun) 1.88	
	G André (FRA) 1.88	

Standing HJ

R Ewry (USA) 1.57	K Tsiklitiras (Gre) 1.55	–

Pole Vault

E Cooke (USA) 3.70	–	E Archibald (CAN) 3.58
A Gilbert (USA) 3.70		B Söderstrom (SWE) 3.58
		C Jacobs (USA) 3.58

Long Jump

F Irons (USA) 7.48	D Kelly (USA) 7.09	C Bricker (CAN) 7.08

Hop, Step and Jump

T Ahearne (GBR) 14.92	G McDonald (CAN) 14.76	E Larsen (NOR) 14.39

Shot

R Rose (USA) 14.21	D Horgan (GBR) 13.61	J Garrels (USA) 13.18

Discus

M Sheridan (USA) 40.89	M Griffin (USA) 40.70	M Horr (USA) 39.44

Discus (Greek Style)

M Sheridan (USA) 38.00	M Horr (USA) 37.325	W Järvinen (FIN) 36.48

Hammer

J Flanagan (USA) 51.92	M McGrath (USA) 51.18	C Walsh (CAN) 48.50

Javelin

E Lemming (SWE) 54.82	A Halse (NOR) 50.57	O Nilsson (SWE) 47.09

Javelin (Free Style)

E Lemming (SWE) 54.445	M Dorizas (Gre) 51.36	A Halse (NOR) 49.73

3 Miles Team Race

GBR 6 pts	USA 19	FRA 32

3500 metres Walk

G Larner (GBR) 14:55.0	E Webb (GBR) 15:07.4	H Kerr (Nzl) 15:43.4
		J Biller (USA) 1.55m

Boxing

Bantamweight

H Thomas (GBR)	J Condon (GBR)	W Webb (GBR)

Featherweight

R Gunn (GBR)	C Morris (GBR)	H Roddin (GBR)

Lightweight

F Grace (GBR)	F Spiller (GBR)	H Johnson (GBR)

Middleweight

J Douglas (GBR)	R Baker (Aus/nzl)	W Philo (GBR)

Heavyweight

A Oldman GBR)	S Evans (GBR)	F Parks (GBR)

Cycling

4000 Metres Team Pursuit

GBR 2:18.6	GER 2:28.6	CAN 2:29.6

660 Yards Track (603.5m)

V Johnson (GBR) 51.2	E Demangel (FRA) Close	K Neumer (GER) 1 lgth

5000 Metres Track
B Jones (GBR) 8:36.2   M Schilles (FRA)   A Auffray (FRA)
20,000 Metres Track
C Kingsbury (GBR) 34:13.6 B Jones (GBR)   J Werbrouck (Bel)
100 Kilometres Track
C Bartlett (GBR) 2h 41:48.6 C Denny (GBR)   O Lapize (FRA)

Fencing

Épée
G Alibert (FRA) 5 wins   A Lippmann (FRA) 4   E Olivier (FRA) 4
Team Épée
FRA   GBR   BEL
Sabre
J Fuchs (HUN) 6 wins   B Zulavsky (HUN) 6   V Von Lobsdorf (BOH) 4
Team Sabre
HUN   ITA   BOH

Football

GBR   DEN   HOL

Gymnastics

Team
SWE 438   NOR 425   FIN 405
Individual Combined Exercises
A Braglia (ITA) 317.0   S W Tysal (GBR) 312.0   L Ségura (FRA) 297.0

Hockey

ENG   IRE   SCO & WAL

Rowing

Single Sculls
H Blackstaffe (GBR) 9:26.0 A McCulloch (GBR)1 Lgth   B Von Gaza (GER) Dna
                                                         K Levitsky (HUN) Dna
Coxless Pairs
GBR 9:43.0   GBR 2.5 Lengths   CAN & GER
Fours
GBR 8:34.0   GBR 1.5 Lengths   NET & CAN
Eights
GBR I 7:52.0   BEL 2 Lengths   GBR & CAN

Yachting

6 Metres
GBR   BEL   FRA
8 Metres
GBR   SWE   GBR
12 Metres
GBR   GBR   –

Statistics

Shooting

Rapid-fire Pistol
P Van Asbroeck (BEL) 490 | R Storms (BEL) 487 | J Gorman (USA) 485

Small-bore Rifle – (Prone)
A Carnell (GBR) 387 | H Humby (GBR) 386 | G Barnes (GBR) 385

Olympic Trap Shooting
Single Shot
S Merlin (GBR) 15 | A Metaxas (RE) 13 | G Merlin (GBR) 12

Double Shot
W Ewing (CAN) 72 | G Beattie (CAN) 60 | A Maunder (GBR) 57
| | A Metaxas (GRE) 57

Free Rifle (Three Positions)
A Helgerud (NOR) 909 | H Simon (USA) 887 | O Saether (NOR) 883

Free Rifle
J Millner (GBR) 98 | K Casey (USA) 93 | M Blood (GBR) 92

Free Rifle (Team)
NOR 5055 | SWE 4711 | FRA 4652

Military Rifle (Team)
USA 2531 | GBR 2497 | CAN 2439

Small Bore Rifle
Moving Target
J Fleming (GBR) 24 | M Matthews (GBR) 24 | W Marsden (GBR) 24

Disappearing Target
W Styles (GBR) 45 | H Hawkins (GBR) 45 | E Amoore (GBR) 45

Small Bore Rifle (Team)
GBR 771 | SWE 737 | FRA 710

Clay Pigeon (Team)
GBR 407 | CAN 405 | GBR 372

Running Deer Shooting
Single Shot
O Swahn (SWE) 25 | T Ranken (GBR) 24 | A Rogers (GBR) 24

Double Shot
W Winans (USA) 46 | T Ranken (GBR) 46 | O Swahn (SWE) 38

Running Deer Shooting (Team)
SWE 86 | GBR 85 | –

Team Event
USA 1914 | BEL 1863 | GBR 1817

Swimming

100 Metres Freestyle
C Daniels (USA) 1:05.6 | Z Halmay (HUN) 1:06.2 | H Julin (SWE) 1:08.0

400 Metres Freestyle
H Taylor (GBR) 5:36.8 | F Beaurepaire (Aus) 5:44.2 | O Scheff (AUT) 5:46.0

1500 Metres Freestyle
H Taylor (GBR) 22:48.4 | S Battersby (GBR) 22:51.2 | F Beaurepaire (AUS)
22:56.2

200 Metres Breaststroke
F Holman (GBR) 3:09.2 | W Robinson (GBR) 3:12.8 | P Hansson (SWE) 3:14.6

100 Metres Backstroke
A Bieberstein (GER) 1:24.6 | L Dam (Den) 1:26.6 | H Haresnape (GBR) 1:27.0

171

4x200 Metres Freestyle Relay
GBR 10:55.6   HUN 10:59.0   USA 11:02.8

Diving

Springboard
A Turner (GER) 85.5   K Behrens (GER) 85.3   G Giadzik (USA) 80.8
G Walz (GER) 80.8

Platform
H Johansson (SWE) 83.75   K Malmström (SWE) 78.73   A Spangberg (SWE) 74.00

Water Polo

GBR   BEL   SWE

Tennis

Men
Singles
J Ritchie (GBR)   O Froitzheim (GER)   W Eves (GBR)
Doubles
GBR   GBR   GBR
GBR   GBR   SWE
Women
Singles
D Chambers (GBR)   D Boothby (GBR)   J Winch (GBR)
G Eastlake-Smith (GBR)   A Greene (GBR)   M Adlerstrahle (SWE)

Wrestling

Free-style
Bantamweight
G Mehnert (USA)   W Press (GBR)   A Coté (CAN)
Featherweight
G Dole (USA)   J Slim (GBR)   W Mckie (GBR)
Lightweight
G De Relwyskow (GBR)   W Wood (GBR)   A Gingell (GBR)
Middleweight
S Bacon (GBR)   G De Relwyskow (GBR)   F Beck (GBR)
Light-heavyweight
V Weckman (FIN)   Y Saarala (FIN)   C Jensen (DEN)
Heavyweight
G O'kelly (GBR)   J Gundersen (NOR)   E Barrett (GBR)
Greco Roman
Lightweight
E Porro (ITA)   N Orlov (RUS)   Avid Lindén-Linko (FIN)
Middleweight
A Märtensson (SWE)   M Andersson (SWE)   A Andersen (DEN)
Heavyweight
R Weisz (HUN)   A Petrov (RUS)   S Jensen (Den)

Jeu De Paume

J Gould (USA)   E Mills (GBR)   N Lytton (GBR)

Lacrosse

| CAN | GBR | – |

Motorboating

Open Class
| FRA | – | – |

60 Foot Class
| GBR | – | – |

8 Metre Class
| GBR | – | – |

Polo

| GBR | GBR | GBR |

Rackets

Singles
| E Noel (GBR) | H Leaf (GBR) | J Jacob Astor (GBR) |

Doubles
| GBR | GBR | GBR |

Rugby Union

| Australia | GBR | – |

Tug Of War

| GBR | GBR | GBR |

Gold Medals by Sports and Countries

	GBR	USA	SWE	FRA	GER	HUN	CAN	NOR	ITA	BEL	AUS/NZ	RUS	FIN	SA	Total
Archery	2			1											3
Athletics	8	16	2				1							1	28
Boxing	5														5
Cycling	5			1											6
Fencing				2		2									4
Figure Skating	1		1		1							1			4
Football	1														1
Gymnastics			1						1						2
Hockey	1														1
Real Tennis		1													1
Lacrosse							1								1
Polo	1														1
Rackets	2														2
Rugby											1				1
Rowing	4														4
Sailing	4														4
Shooting	6	3	2				1	2		1					15
Swimming/Diving	5	1	1		2										9
Tennis	6														6
Water Motorsports	2			1											3
Wrestling	3	2	1			1			1				1		9
Total	**56**	**23**	**8**	**5**	**3**	**3**	**3**	**2**	**2**	**1**	**1**	**1**	**1**	**1**	**110**

Source: Mallon and Buchanan

Annotated Bibliography

There are two indispensable primary sources of information covering specifically the 1908 London Games. *The Official Report of The Olympic Games of 1908* was drawn up by Theodore Cook and published in 1909 by the British Olympic Council. This comprehensive work includes a complete list of competitors and results, photographs of winners, information on the preparations for the Games and comments of most of the events of the Games. It contains also the rules and regulations governing each Sport. The other very good primary source of information is the book coauthored by the Olympic historians Bill Mallon and Ian Buchanan, *The 1908 Olympic Games* (Jefferson NC, 2000) which covers the results of all competitions together with a commentary on them. The book also provides some interesting material dealing with the disputes and protests that arose during and after the Games.

Several general histories of the modern Olympics have been written which include particularly useful information on the 1908 Games. The pick of the bunch are David Wallechinsky's, *The Complete Book of the Olympics* (New York 991), John Findling's and Kimberly Pelle's, *Historical Dictionary of the Modern Olympic Movement* (Westport, Conn.1996), *The Olympic Games*, edited by Lord Killanin and John

Rodda (London 1979), Frederick Webster's *Olympic Cavalcade* (London 1948), and Allen Guttman's, *The Olympics*, (Chicago 2002). Brian Dobbs includes an interesting chapter on the revival of the Olympian movement in his book, *Edwardians at Play* (London 1973).

Richard Schaap in his impressive, *Illustrated History of the Olympics*, (New York 1975), covers the 1908 Games and highlights the Marathon event. Another well documented history of the early Olympics can be found in John Kieran's and Arthur Daley's *The Story of the Olympic Games 776 B.C.-1952 A.D.* (Philadelphia 1969) Readers interested in the political background to the Games will find this aspect covered well in David Kanin's, *Political History of the Olympic Games*, (Boulder, Colo. 1981). On a lighter note, William Johnson's, *All that Glitters is not Gold* (New York 1972) and David Guiney's, *The Dunlop Book of the Olympics*, (Lavenham 1975) both provide an amusing and irreverent look at the Olympics in general, and feature incidents and athletes from the London Games.

There are three useful sources of information dealing specifically with the Games' controversies. George Matthews in his article, *The Controversial Olympic Games of 1908*, provides a good insight into how the disputes were regarded in the press on both sides of the Atlantic, (Journal of Sports History 1980). Similarly, Caspar Whitney has covered this aspect judiciously in the American sporting weekly, *Outing* magazine. As regards the role and influence of the Irish American athletes and officials, this is described well in John Schaefer's, *The Irish American Athletic Club: Redefining Americanism at the 1908 Olympic Games*, (Archives of Irish Americans). Thomas Burlford provides a British perspective in his, *American Hatred and British Folly*, (London 1911)

Only a few of the Olympians portrayed in this book have been the subject of specific published biographies. By far the most detailed is Greg Growden's thorough and colourful account of Snowy Baker's eventful life in his book, *The Snowy Baker Story*, (Netley, South Australia 2003). The astonishing career of Tom Longboat is dealt with perceptively in Bruce Kidd's biography, *Tom Longboat*, (Markham, Ontario 2004), and also by David Blaikie on the Internet –www.davidblaikie. com. The Sheridan Memorial Community Centre at Bohola, Ireland, has compiled a warm and thorough account of Martin Sheridan's life and illustrious athletic career in its publication, *The Martin Sheridan Story* (c1999)

Otherwise, most of the biographical information used is drawn from a variety of sources, such as books, articles and newspapers and the Internet. Many of the accounts of the 1908 Games refer to the inspirational role played by Lord Desborough, although he has yet to receive the full biography he deserves. However, readers can find a useful summary of his remarkable sporting achievements in the publication *Olympic Hero* (Taplow Court 1994). Similarly, the illustrious marathon runners Johnny

Hayes and Dorando Pietri both lack thorough biographies, although a wealth of personal and anecdotal details appears in various books, articles, and internet sites when their part in the London Marathon is discussed. Relatively little has been published about the Olympic champions Ralph Rose, Madge Syers and Henry Taylor, but James Bancroft has included a much-needed sketch of the life and achievements of the swimmer Henry Taylor in his publication, *Olympic Champions* in *Manchester* (Aim High Publications 1993)

Reports on the Games were carried in several British newspapers and magazines but the best daily coverage can be found in *The Times* for the period July 13-25, 1908. The British published a daily sporting newspaper, *The Sporting Life*, during the Games, and also in 1908 produced a complete record of the winners and events. The American newspapers such as the *New York Times*, the *New York Herald* and the *New York Daily Sun*, also maintained a high interest in the Games both during and after the event, and especially in the controversies that arose.

About the author

Keith Baker is a former senior civil servant, and a historian and sports devotee by temperament. He has worked as a journalist and has just completed a book on the famous Yorkshire chemist and philosopher Joseph Priestley.

His interest in the Olympics was first inspired as a boy when the Games came to London in 1948, and he has become fascinated by the sporting achievements of the great Olympians and their lives subsequently.

Other books from SportsBooks

The 1948 Olympics – How London Rescued the Games
Bob Phillips
ISBN 9781899807 54 3
£16.99 (hardback)

London was far from the obvious candidate to stage the
1948 Olympic Games. The country was still suffering the
after effects of the war. Rationing was in operation. Bomb
sites remained throughout the city. Yet London took on the
Games and staged them very successfully.
Athletes were housed in barracks and schools and were
given tickets for the underground to make their own way
to the stadium. Those British athletes who lived in or near
London stayed at home. Among the 1948 champions are
some of the legendary figures of Olympic sport – Fanny
Blankers-Koen, Emil Zatopek, Bob Mathias (all athletics),
Luszlo Papp (boxing), Sammy Lee (diving), Burnell and
Bushnell (rowing), Willy Grut (modern pentathlon).

Stan Greenberg's Olympic Almanack 2008
ISBN 9781899807 53 6
£14.99 (paperback)

The most authoritative and enjoyable collection of Olympic
facts, records, anecdotes and statistics from the ancient
Games right up to the present. Now in its seventh edition,
after previously being published by Guinness and Whitaker's,
the Almanack includes profiles of every summer and winter
Olympic Games; summaries of Olympic history, sports,
events, people and performances and medal tables by sport
and year.

Arthur Lydiard Master Coach
Garth Gilmour
ISBN 1899807 22 5
£17.99 (hardback)

Arthur Lydiard, who died at the end of 2004, was probably
the most successful and influential running coach of the
twentieth century. Garth Gilmour, Lydiard's close friend for
more than forty years, tells for the first time the full story of the
coach's amazing career, often in Lydiard's own words.

From Sheffield with Love
Brendan Murphy
ISBN 9781899807 56 7
£8.99 (paperback)

Sheffield FC, the world's oldest football club, celebrated
its 150th anniversary in 2007. But this book does not only
celebrate the birth of the club known simply as "The Club".
It also traces the growth of organised football which took
place in Sheffield in the latter part of the nineteenth century.
For a while the Sheffield Football Association rivalled
the Football Association to be the arbiters of the game.
But gradually the two sets of laws were amalgamated.
Sheffield, though, can claim to be the birthplace of football.